THE FIRST

AND

FINEST

THE FIRST AND FINEST

ORTHODOX CHRISTIAN STEWARDSHIP
AS
SACRED OFFERING

Rev. Fr. Robert Holet, DMin.

authorHOUSE®

AuthorHouse™ LLC
1663 Liberty Drive
Bloomington, IN 47403
www.authorhouse.com
Phone: 1-800-839-8640

Published by AuthorHouse   11/04/2013

ISBN: 978-1-4918-2136-7 (sc)
ISBN: 978-1-4918-2135-0 (e)

Library of Congress Control Number: 2013917740

CONTENTS

To the Glory of God
In the Year of Our Lord
2013

PREFACE

When a student completes a doctoral program, he or she is often asked, "What will you do now?" Often the answer comes quickly, "Publish a book!" From that fine tradition emerges this work!

On a more serious note, my study of Orthodox Christian stewardship, in the course of my Doctor of Ministry studies at Pittsburgh Theological Seminary and the Antiochian House of Studies (2006), challenged me both personally and professionally. I've concluded that the topic of Orthodox Stewardship is *both central to a contemporary understanding of Orthodoxy today, and often misunderstood*. As Director of the Consistory Office of Stewardship of the Ukrainian Orthodox Church of the USA (*UOCofUSA*), I've had the privilege of speaking to many people about stewardship in a way that has helped to form some of the content in this book. My conclusion is an awareness that the foundational understanding emerging from a study of Orthodox stewardship must lead to an Orthodox *practice* of stewardship. The intent of this book is to serve as a tool which helps to form the reader's understanding of Orthodox stewardship—fostered in Orthodox Holy Tradition, leading to spiritual awareness and faithfulness in his or her stewardship, and mindful of the multitude of God's gifts entrusted to each of us.

This book is intended to fill a pastoral need through a discussion of stewardship themes that emerge from the two "fonts" of Christian truth - the Bible and Christian Tradition. These "streams" water the Christian Church and the human soul to live fully in the Christian life—with the grace of the Holy Spirit, as good and faithful servants.[1] As with most such efforts to translate a doctoral paper to a more popular audience, I have changed certain aspects of the content of the original paper, adding some new material and reworking certain sections. The final section offers one schema for a parish Orthodox stewardship program. Despite this work's academic origins, I hope that the effort to rework the material allows the discussion to flow easily enough for most readers.

About the Stewardship Project

Because a Doctor of Ministry paper typically is more than a purely academic paper,[2] it also incorporates an interactive project in the service of others, where theoretical concepts are presented and tested in a ministry setting. Most of the content of the project itself has been excised from this book, but can be accessed in the original doctoral paper or by request. This work will focus more on the concepts underlying Orthodox Stewardship rather than the details of how they were applied in the mission parish stewardship project. Nevertheless, most of the conclusions in the final section of this work will speak from the understanding garnered from the entire project.

Why Study Orthodox Stewardship?

The practice of financial stewardship has a profound effect on spiritual and practical dimensions of personal sanctity and Church life. My awareness of this effect grew as a result of challenges posed both in the Ukrainian Orthodox mission parish in Charlottesville, Virginia which I serve as well as in the broader ecclesiastical context of Orthodoxy in America.[3]

Initially, when I was entrusted by my hierarch to start the mission parish, it was necessary to gather basic personal and financial resources to be able to celebrate liturgical services, promote the new mission locally and begin the work of shaping a parish community.[4] In June of 1998, shortly after we began to celebrate our first services in a hotel space, the parish was blessed to welcome several new members who spoke of the practice of tithing, having learned the practice as Protestant Christians.[5] In addition to helping the parish financially, their practice of tithing gave witness to a certain biblical orientation in financial offering. Their example raised fundamental questions; for example, what is the nature of spiritual and monetary offering in the Orthodox Church? Are there guidelines for financial giving in the Orthodox Church? Is the practice of tithing either required of Orthodox Christians or even advantageous? Later, in my presentations to clergy and laity as Director of the Office of

Stewardship in the Ukrainian Orthodox Church of the USA, these same questions were raised frequently, sometimes vociferously.

The establishment of our new mission parish also raised fundamental questions for me about how *the Church as a whole* was to fund newly-established mission parishes.[6] Was the congregation to be funded through more customary means - parish membership dues and fundraising efforts - or through a model of giving characterized by free will offerings and the implementation of a stewardship/ tithing model?[7] How did other mission parishes work through this issue? Should startup parishes be planted and funded by the central administration of the Orthodox jurisdiction or from local resources?

A Broader Ecclesiastical Context

The question was further prompted by a personal experience attending the Sobor of the Ukrainian Orthodox Church of the USA in 1998.[8] Many discussions during the Sobor sessions revolved around certain core issues that had very little to do with the spiritual mission of the Church. The troubled sentiment of many participants during these discussions stood in stark contrast to a fundamentally positive and joyous Christian vision, based in trust of God as the Source of "every good and perfect gift" as was celebrated in the Liturgies of the same Sobor.[9] Some delegates were concerned about the very survival of the Church because of financial matters. Much time and effort was exhausted in wrangling over financial issues, leaving precious little time to deal with other core issues of Church life such as catechesis, leadership, evangelization, youth ministry, liturgical and parish life, etc.[10] I came to the realization during this time that a preoccupation with financial concerns could easily undermine any efforts to advance the spiritual activities that would deepen church member commitment to God and His Church. This fearful preoccupation, in the end, could undermine the financial bottom line as well.

Further reflection has raised additional questions. Are financial problems practical or spiritual in nature? Are financial issues in parish life symptomatic of hidden spiritual issues confronting the Church?

If that is the case, what comprises true *Orthodox* stewardship? Are there essential elements in an Orthodox approach that make it fundamentally different from contemporary Protestant or Roman Catholic approaches? Are personal and parish stewardship practices (or those of the Church at large) fundamentally inconsistent with the spiritual norms of an *Orthodox* Christian approach to stewardship, as presented in scripture and Holy Tradition?

A significant percentage of the income in many established Orthodox parishes in the United States is derived from member dues, which serve as a type of ecclesiastical per capita assessment that funds local parish activities. In some cases, constitutions of the Orthodox Church jurisdictions define a "dues system" for parishes, where a fixed per capita amount is to be sent to the administrative body of jurisdiction's central administration offices to meet the broader needs of the Church.[11]

Reflecting on this system of member dues, one might wonder why it was so common, and how it influenced parish life. In parishes where the dues system was normative, did the models of parish leadership, administration of funds, and relational interactions tend to be based on a capitalistic business model - where there may be a temptation to equate money with control and power?[12] This 'run the parish as a business' approach may be juxtaposed to the spirit of selfless Christian generosity, proceeding from an awareness that what one has been given comes from God Himself. Such generosity should prompt the dispersal of these financial resources through acts of Christian love and service.[13] A pragmatic or secular vision, with its resultant practices, could do nothing to remedy spiritually toxic attitudes of avarice, lust for power, obstinacy, resentment, spiritual dualism and a host of other evils that can poison parish life and by extension the entire ecclesiastical matrix. These questions and observations prompt an exploration of the spiritual and practical dynamics of financial giving in Orthodox parishes.

Stewardship Resources for Orthodox Christians

The norms for Orthodox Christian behavior (individual and corporate) are found in the revelation of Christ in the Holy Scriptures and in Holy Tradition.[14] In Orthodoxy, Holy Tradition is viewed as the ongoing work of the Holy Spirit prompting the Church to live the truth embodied in the teachings of Christ, as implemented throughout the two millennia of Orthodox Christianity.[15] A true Orthodox approach to stewardship will integrate elements of an Orthodox understanding of the subject as gleaned from the liturgical life of the Church, canonical guidelines, patristic teachings, iconography, architectural structures, etc. which reveal biblical truths over the course of their development in Church history.[16] This project has explored, in a cursory way, some of these theoretical elements in order to construct a pastoral approach to Orthodox stewardship as it is lived in parishes of twenty-first century United States.

For this writing, the theme of *liturgical offering as the basis of stewardship* will serve as the theological thread which knits together the ongoing *praxis* of the Orthodox Church in history. In Orthodoxy, the notion of *offering* is linked to the Church's participation in the offering of Christ "in behalf of all [humans] and for all [things]" in the context of the Eucharistic liturgy.[17] However, offering is also reflected by the tangible contributions of the faithful, exemplified in freewill financial offerings, offerings of bread, wine, oil, etc. for liturgical use, special need offerings including charity for the poor, first fruits offerings (particularly those presented on the Feast of the Transfiguration), personal offerings to the priest, and countless other examples.[18] Some offerings, like the offering of one's time and talent, encompass other aspects of giving.[19] The importance of worship in Orthodoxy is obvious as the very term 'Orthodoxy' means 'right worship'.[20] Hence offering is linked integrally to worship/liturgy and the proper glorification of God with one's being—body and soul. In Orthodoxy, this will manifest itself primarily through corporate liturgical worship of the Church as a body.[21]

Through the examination of the theory and practice of Orthodox stewardship in parishes, the basis for Orthodox Christian stewardship can be better understood. Developing a method to present Orthodox stewardship in a parish context can then be an effective tool for pastoral ministry—leading God's people to a deeper life of Christian holiness.

Acknowledgements

Clearly, this work has been a work of many years and influenced by many who are close to me personally, as well as others whom the Lord has brought into my life perhaps for but a moment, who nonetheless profoundly influenced my thought on this subject. I do wish to acknowledge specifically my hierarchs of the Ukrainian Orthodox Church of the USA:, His Eminence Metropolitan +Antony, and His Grace Bishop +Daniel who have provided opportunities to explore the topic of stewardship in ministry in many aspects of Church life, as well as thoughtful critiques on my approach to this work. My readers for the original doctoral project, Dr. Edith M. Humphrey (Pittsburgh Theological Seminary) and V. Rev. Fr. Nicholas Ferencz, provided not only formative guidance but also helpful resources and essential editing to the original doctoral project paper.

The faithful of St. Nicholas Parish in Charlottesville (Greenwood), Virginia have served as a remarkable witness to the spirit of sacrificial offering which has made visible to me the true character of Orthodox stewardship through their financial offerings, as well as the offering of their time, talent and trust in the parish context. My experience of sacrificial stewardship reaches much further back into my personal past, when I reflect on the love of the Church embodied by the people of St. Nicholas Byzantine Catholic Church in Perryopolis, Pennsylvania. Their stewardship of the Faith affirmed that which I experienced daily, especially through the profound love of my parents, the late Michael Holet and my mother, Pauline Holet.

These are all strands of life experience and belief, but they have been tied together for me through my relationship with my loving wife, Pani Matka Christine Holet. Not only does Christine daily exemplify the principles of offering and worship in stewardship at Church, but in the ministry to God in His Church and love of others, and of me. She was instrumental at every stage of the doctoral project, including practical things such as the editing of this manuscript, but also in its embedded thought.

With the spirit of Thanksgiving, may God be glorified in these words, to the edification of His people.

PART I

Old Testament Foundations
Stewardship and Offering

The Offerings of Cain and Abel
St. Sophia Seminary - South Bound Brook, NJ

CHAPTER ONE

THE BOOK OF GENESIS

The Sacrificial and Sacramental Character of Human Life

Orthodox Christianity incorporates an understanding of the nature of the human person and one's relationship with God into every aspect of its theology and worship, including the concept of stewardship.[1] Orthodox Christian anthropology is based on a vision of the rightful place of humanity in the order of creation, and illuminates key dimensions of Orthodox worship, doctrine and Church life. The following serve as essential elements of this vision: the creation of man by God as eternally good, the corruption of the relationship of God and humankind (and creation) as a result of the sin of Adam, the punishment of God including death and expulsion from paradise, and the disorder of human life after the fall, including inclination toward sinful passions.[2] This vision of humanity not only describes the fallen human state, but also points to the restorative, salvific work within human beings accomplished by the God-man, Jesus Christ.[3]

In this context, the word 'stewardship' can be defined as *a right and holy human interaction with other human beings and with creation itself, carried out as a fruit of humankind's relationship with God.* The first humans were created by God and set as stewards over all creation, being given the authority to name the species of plants and animals as a sign of that authority and unique dignity, reflecting the very image and likeness of God Himself.[4]

In Eden, God planted the garden and gave to Adam and Eve their very being and all that they needed (Gen. 2:8ff). The whole of creation was a manifestation of the providential and intimate love of God and intended as a means through which humans could commune with God in love, thanksgiving and joy. However, instead of cherishing their relationship with the Creator through

3

their thankful reception and use of creation as coming from Him, and instead of returning thanksgiving to Him, Adam and Eve seized creation as an end in itself. The sinful Fall begins when the first humans fail to recognize their priestly vocation of offering thanksgiving through obedience to God (Gen. 3:1-7). This sin is a manifestation of pride and disobedience in the human heart, and the result is a cataclysmic rupture in the relationship between God and humanity, and humanity and creation.[5] The fallen human will orients itself toward matter as an end in itself; the human vocation to intimacy with God, characterized by thanksgiving, is thereby destroyed. This discord results in the punishment of death, where the human body itself is subsumed in the very matter of creation, and no longer exercises stewardship over it.

Orthodoxy views the human fall as tragic, but not ultimate. God continued to visit humankind with His mercy throughout time, particularly in the Covenant with Abraham and his descendents.[6] The saving work culminates in restoration of humankind in Christ, the new Adam - who as the Son of God takes flesh, ultimately destroying the curse of the tree of Eden and death itself, through *His* death on the tree of the Cross and by His resurrection. Fr. Alexander Schmemann notes that,

> The first, the basic definition of man is that he is *priest*. He stands in the center of the world and unifies it in his act of blessing God, of both receiving the world from God and offering it to God - and by filling the world with this eucharist, he transforms his life, the one that he receives from the world, into life in God, into communion with Him. The world was created as the "matter," the material of one all-embracing Eucharist, and man was created as the priest of this cosmic sacrament.[7]

It follows that this priestly action of offering and sanctification requires both matter—the stuff of the earth which is to be offered - and a spiritual action in the heart. The sin of humankind was and continues to be a failure of stewardship, and a rejection of this original priestly vocation. All of Orthodox doctrine and worship is

4

permeated by the awareness that humanity bears this priestly dignity. The Paschal sacrifice of the Incarnate Christ is salvific because He, in obedience, submission and thanksgiving, offers Himself perfectly to the Father.[8] Communion with God is restored in His very being. The Church celebrates this Eucharist by offering thanksgiving in obedience, remembering "all that was done for our sake."[9] The sacramental restoration of communion with God becomes a model for all of life, and rediscovery of the priestly vocation—the offerings of creation back to God in thanksgiving. This is *human* stewardship. Hence, the priestly vocation is not to be limited to a clerical cult, but is to be characteristic of all human activity.

Offerings and the Human Heart: The Stewardship of Cain and Abel

If the human vocation is priestly in nature, it is no coincidence that the depth of human brokenness was made manifest shortly after the expulsion of Adam and Eve from Paradise (Gen. 3) through the offering of an unacceptable religious sacrifice.[10] The story of Cain and Abel is, in the end, a religious story of the beauty and glory of the righteous sacrifice, juxtaposed to an unworthy religious sacrifice which falls short of pleasing God, spawning the sin of despondency and resulting in murder.[11] This Yahwistic account[12] describes the unacceptable offering of the mere "produce of the soil" offered by Cain, compared to the "first-born of his flock and some of their fat as well" offered by Abel, which was looked upon with favor by the Lord (Gen.4:3f).[13]

The Orthodox understanding of this passage arises from a comparison between the two offerings as to their *inner* quality, reflective of the inner state of heart of those who made the offerings. Cain's failure is precisely a failure to offer the 'first' and the 'best'. St. John Chrysostom notes the importance of the distinction between the two offerings:

> "Cain," the text says, "brought an offering of the fruits of the earth to the Lord"; then, wanting to teach us about Abel as

well, Sacred Scripture says that he for his part also brought his offering from his occupation and his shepherding. "He, for his part, also brought an offering," the text says, remember, "of the firstborn of his flock, and in fact the fattest of them." Notice how it hints to us of the piety of this man's attitude, and the fact that he did not casually offer any one of his sheep, but "one of the firstborn," that is, from the valuable and special ones. In Cain's case, on the contrary, nothing of the kind is suggested; rather, the fact that he brought "an offering of the fruits of the earth," as if to say, whatever came to hand, without any display of zeal or precise care.[14]

For Chrysostom, the reason for the rejection of Cain's offering is that it is made with carelessness and lack of zeal. This careless state of *heart* is what is at the root of the problem, not the sacrifice itself. When the offering of Cain is found to be unacceptable, the passage describes the dialog of Cain with the Lord, further revealing the shift of the inner disposition of his heart toward despondency.[15] From this inner attitude proceeds a second, terrible sin—jealousy - which leads to Cain's murder by his brother Abel. Note that the curse of Cain, the tiller of the earth, strikes at the very heart of his life's work as a tiller of the soil, and is also related to the curse of his father Adam: "When you till the ground it shall no longer yield you any of its produce." (Gen. 4:13; Gen. 3:17-19)

Among the many lessons of this passage, four observations can be made. First, the sacrificial orientation of man is present in his very nature, evidenced by both Cain and Abel, from the first passages in the Bible. Their relationships with God, even as sons of the fallen Adam, are not utterly shattered by the Fall. There is no sense in this passage of their sacrificial offerings as appeasements of an angry God who threatened to deprive them of the material necessities for their lives.[16] Rather, it is evident that the earth had continued to produce sufficiently for Cain - the curse of his father Adam notwithstanding - so that he could make an offering to the Lord. Throughout Genesis, the offering of sacrifices by the patriarchs is evidence of a dynamic faith in God and a living relationship with Him.

Secondly, the passage introduces the deeply biblical notion of offering the *first fruits* - an important aspect of the sacrificial tradition of later Judaism which would also form a basis for subsequent Christian worship and Eucharistic theology.[17] That Abel would offer the *first* of his flock indicated an orientation to offer the best, the finest, and the first to God. At a typological level of interpretation, the patristic tradition saw the acceptable offering of the first born by Abel as a type of the offering of Christ.[18]

Thirdly, the failure to offer worthy sacrifice is an external manifestation of sin in the heart. In the case of Cain, the sin of carelessness would lead to inner despondency and a further strain in his relational dialog with God. This problem between Cain and his God spills over into his relationship with his brother, prompting jealousy. As a result, Cain kills his brother. Furthermore, as a result of his actions, fear seized his heart; to avoid retribution for his actions, Cain wandered the earth in *fear* - further destroying his vocation as a 'tiller of the earth.'[19] Apparently, there are high stakes regarding the offerings and their acceptability to God, and the importance of offering with a right inner disposition.

Finally, when a sacrificial offering is made in a righteous manner, it is acceptable to God and leads to a communion—with the one who offers and God. The offering is a celebration of God's sustaining love and providence, being quintessentially relational—a hearkening back to the original communion of God and humankind in paradise. For Christians, this offering prefigures the return and restoration of the original relationship of God and humankind accomplished in Christ. In Orthodoxy, this sense of sacrifice and communion would be integrally linked to the fuller understanding of the paschal offering of Christ and the Eucharist as a Holy Communion.[20]

The Offering to Melchizedek - the Priest and King

Abram's offering of the tithe to Melchizedek is interpreted by the Orthodox Church as a model of the right stewardship of earthly offerings and the prefigurement of the offering of Christ, the King of Peace (Salem), as the perfect offering.[21] In the Genesis narrative,

Abram has returned from a victory in battle over Chedor-laomer and his allies, and he has received the spoils of such a major victory. When Melchizedek appears, bringing a priestly offering of bread and wine, he blesses Abram. In response, Abram offers a tenth (tithe) of everything. In certain aspects of Hebraic thought, material wealth was viewed as a sign of the favor of God, whereas impoverishment was viewed as evidence of God's judgment of sin. Hence, the victory was a sign of God's blessing and guidance to Abram, a material offering shared with Melchizedek, the priest and king.

The author of Hebrews develops the Christian theology of the priesthood of Christ on behalf of all humankind, through an interpretation of the Melchizedek encounter as a type of Christ, "You are a priest forever according to the order of Melchizedek." (Heb. 7:17)[22] The offering of Abram links several key elements of sacrifice to the stewardship of goods. First, the offering is made in a liturgical/religious context, in *thanksgiving* for the blessing imparted, and, more broadly, for the victory over the enemy.

In the Orthodox Christian typological interpretation of this passage, the liturgical-priestly dimension of worship manifest in Hebrews, and the succession of Christ as High Priest and Prince of Peace set the context for all subsequent human offerings and for our stewardship of creation. Abraham (Abram), the great Patriarch, offers the tithe to the priest-king Melchizedek, signifying that he is greater in dignity than Abraham (Heb. 7:6). The offering serves as a prefiguration of the eternal sacrifice offered by the messianic High Priest. In Hebrews, additional offerings and tithes are no longer offered for sin as in the practice of the Old Covenant, for the High Priest, Christ, has made a sacrificial offering of His Body, once and for all. It is the Body of the Lamb of God, which is the perfect offering acceptable to the Father.[23]

An important aspect of the Melchizedek passage lies in its chronology. The battle is won with the assistance of God, the mysterious priest-king appears with bread and wine in symbolic offering and so blesses Abram. Then, Abram offers the tithe, in thanksgiving to the priest. Abram's offering is a *response* to the awareness of the deliverance by God, but is prompted by the presence of the priest, who blesses the event and is empowered to receive the offering of thanksgiving. The tithe offering is a response to grace, not a prerequisite of it. There is no sense that Abram's offering is given to appease God or to assure future victories, as might have been typical of certain pagan rituals. There is no evidence that Melchizedek has any need of the offering—the offering is not based on a need or utilitarian purpose, rather it is given freely.[24]

Furthermore, the gift offered by Abram has the characteristic of spontaneity and joy.[25] Orthodox Christianity sees the offering of gifts in the Church as an invitation to a liturgical celebration of freedom, generosity, thanksgiving and joy. The priestly action of Melchizedek points to the priestly action of the Church, where the gifts are received and the blessing of God descends in a liturgical expression of thanksgiving. The joyous response to deliverance is a common theme in the New Testament as well, particularly in the Synoptics; when Christ ministers in the midst of the people, they rejoice and give thanks to God.[26] Joy and communion in the human heart are characteristics of the visitation of God and the acknowledgment of His blessing.

Abraham would also be the central figure in the dramatic story of the offering of His first born son, Isaac - he being the fulfillment in the flesh of God's promise that Abraham would be the "Father of Many Nations" (Gen. 17:5). Nevertheless, Abraham's faithfulness to God would be tested - he would be commanded ascend the mountain with his son, carrying the wood, to be offered as a human sacrifice.[27] The offering would be the sign of faithfulness in stewardship of what was entrusted - essentially offering back to God what had been entrusted to him. God' deliverance is again celebrated in the offering of the replacement ram.

Exemplary Models of the Faithful Stewardship in the Old Testament

Snapshots exist throughout the Pentateuch and Hebrew history, of faithful servants of God, fulfilling His will by faithful offering of themselves and their material and spiritual lives to Him. The

Patriarch Joseph, who is also celebrated in Orthodoxy during Lent and Holy Week as a type of Christ, is one whose life is 'buried' for a time and hidden through the unjust persecution of his brethren. Yet he is spared, and after his faithfulness and purity is tested, he is placed in a situation where his extraordinary gift of interpreting dreams and prophetic insights would lead to his ascent in Egyptian society what could be called the 'Chief Steward' of the land. Again, as part of God's plan, Joseph would be the very one through whom the 'nations' of the promise to Abraham, through Isaac and Jacob, and embodied in Israel's sons, would be delivered from the forthcoming and widespread famine when they journeyed to Egypt, and were reunited with their brother. As the faithful steward abiding in Egypt, Joseph would serve as an example of how the vocation of stewardship would not entirely be limited to later Covenant on Sinai, but rather in the heart wherever one was led. This would be imitated, in the New Testament, by the journey of Jesus to Egypt (Lk. 2), the conversion of the Ethiopian eunuch in Acts (Acts 8:34ff), and the conversion of the Gentiles.

CHAPTER TWO

EXODUS AND BEYOND

The Pattern of Old Testament Stewardship as Offering

The Sacrifice of the Passover and the Covenant

The central events of God's salvation and deliverance in the history of the Hebrew people are found in the narrative of the Exodus and the spiritual leadership of Moses in his confrontation of Pharaoh, the Exodus through the Red Sea, the journey through the desert, and the bestowal of the Covenant. As the spiritual leader of the Hebrews, Moses is the faithful servant of God, in full obedience to His Word, not only through the revelation of the Passover offering of the Lamb, but also through the Eucharistic symbol of the manna from heaven bestowed upon the people. Moses, the prophetic leader in the tradition of the Patriarchs, would direct the elders.[1]

Note that in the Covenant, the leadership roles of Aaron and the elders are related to, but distinct from the prophetic ministry of Moses. The ministry of leadership (the stewardship of the people) would be carried out distinctly as directed by God, by each. In a similar way, Moses would share this ministry of leadership with other elders, called and ordained by God and selected to serve as judges. (Ex. 18:22) The care of the people, exercised through leadership, as exemplified by Joseph a generation or so earlier, would find an ongoing expression according to God's inspiration in the human soul and the grace of God.[2] In the desert, the sacrifice to the golden calf (in the absence of Moses - even as Moses was receiving the tablets of the Law as a sign of the Covenant) served as a sign of the spiritual infidelity of the people and a breakdown in the stewardship/care of the precious relationship bestowed upon the Hebrews by the Lord represented in the Covenant (Ex. 32). In this case, the golden calf offered by the people, as in the case of Cain, revealed the inner disposition of the heart, away from God and toward material things and sensuality of this world, unto their condemnation.

Old Testament Ritual Offerings and the Levitical Tithe

Much of the Pentateuch is replete with liturgical commands given by the Lord, directing the people concerning the proper exercise of their priestly human nature, through a liturgy of offering. These offerings took many forms, including but not limited to grain offerings, sin offerings, burnt offerings, peace offerings, etc. involving grain, animals, incense, etc. The cause, manner, timing and material of the offerings varied were explicitly laid out in the Law as explained in Leviticus, Numbers and Deuteronomy. While the multitude of these offerings cannot be fully explored here, there are several patterns embedded in the offering activities which apply to our study of stewardship.

First, these offerings are *prescribed* by God. They form a substructure of the dynamics of worship and life in the Covenant relationship of the Hebrew people with Him. Offerings were a symbol of *recognition* that "The Lord is God" (Ps. 118: 27) and had directive authority over behaviors through the Law, which they had accepted, which were carried out as a response to God's deliverance of His people through their history. Furthermore, they are *liturgical* - taking place in prescribed ritual ways amid prayers and orderly directives, by those consecrated to perform these works. Note also that the offerings were *sacrificial*.[3] The offering consisted of something of value brought to the priest to be given to the Lord - requiring a 'giving up' of that value to the Lord (and indirectly to the Levites.) The notion of sacrifice - to the giving up of life itself, was a common expression of the totality of offering to God.

The offerings were a visible symbol of the acceptance of the Covenant in the heart, and an affirmation of the Covenant in thanksgiving. Failure of performance of the offerings (or any aspect of the Law) was a sign of a breakdown in the faith relationship with God through the Covenant.

One typical example of the Hebraic offerings was the 'wave offering', prescribed in Leviticus:

And the LORD spoke to Moses, saying, 'Speak to the children of Israel, and say to them, When you be come into the land which I give to you, and shall reap the harvest thereof, then you shall bring a sheaf of the first fruits of your harvest to the priest: And he shall wave the sheaf before the LORD, to be accepted for you: on the morrow after the Sabbath the priest shall wave it.'

(Lev. 23:9f, NIV)

This offering typifies the offering of *firstfruits* in the context of Levitical worship, and is seen above in the offerings of Abel, Cain and Abraham. The prescription of the Law and the Levitical offerings inaugurated an ongoing *liturgy* of offerings - a constant force of prayer and worship in the community orienting it toward the Lord. These were to be carried out 'when you come into the land', long before the establishment of the Temple, but the building of the Temple provided a visible, powerful site for the orientation of such worship which would be renewed in the era of the second Temple.[4]

One of the most important modes of first fruits offering prescribed in the Old Covenant was the *tithe*.[5] Among the many passages in Numbers, Leviticus and Deuteronomy referencing the tithe, the following passage is probably the most concise in explaining this directive.[6] The tithe, as the first ten percent of that received, was seen to belong *to the Lord* (Lev. 27.30). The same is true of the first-born of the clean animals.

You are to seek Yahweh your God only in the place He Himself will choose from among all your tribes to set His name here and give it a home. There you shall bring your holocausts and your sacrifices, your tithes, the offerings from your hands, your votive offerings and your voluntary offerings, the first-born of your herd and flock; there will you eat in the presence of Yahweh your God and be thankful for all that your hands have presented, you and your households blessed by God.[7]

Dt.12:5-7

The offering is characterized by a meal; "...you shall eat in the presence of Yahweh your God..." The attitude of giving is also prescribed—the people are to be *thankful*. Normally, the tithe served as the portion provided by the Lord for the Levites (Num. 18:21-24), who were given no portion of land as an inheritance for themselves.[8] Rather, by the Lord's directive, they were the consecrated priestly servants who received tithes and offerings and, through the exercise of their office, gained a material reward to meet their earthly needs. According to the prescription of the Covenant, the offering of an annual tithe was so important that if someone could not literally transfer his or her wealth, due to distance, it was to be converted to money, so that it could be transported and duly offered (Dt. 14:25). Also, the tithe of the third year was to be given to the widows, the orphans and the poor, emphasizing that the prescriptions of the covenant offerings were to bring special earthly blessings to those in need (Dt. 14:28f).[9]

The commandments of the Covenant regarding offerings and stewardship would take on a new dimension with the construction and consecration of the Temple. The notion of a locus for the 'acceptable sacrifice' was based in the promise to Abraham of old, in bringing forth a special nation that would find their rightful *place* in the Promised Land.[10] The consecration of places for prescribed worship (and only worship) as well as the consecration of the servants of God tasked to perform the temple worship served as a matrix for the ongoing means by which the Hebrew people fulfilled their responsibilities to the Covenant. It was the way in which they not only recognized, but carried out, through actions, their own consecration to the Lord. Hence the offering of the first-born son according to the Law, through the priesthood, as well as whole of Judaic ritual, would affirm the Covenant and purify the people through their rites.

Examples of Stewardship and Offering in the Prophets and Wisdom Literature

If the very identity of the Hebrew people and their way of life was formed as recounted in the Pentateuch, the balance of the Hebrew scriptures tell the story of the fidelity of the Hebrew people to this sacred Covenant established by God. Stewardship of material blessings from God and fidelity in making offerings would play a key role in the manifestation of the Covenant in daily life. The ministry of leadership, as stewardship of the people, was a critical component of this history of Israel. Whenever the leaders were faithful to the Covenant, the people were blessed. When unfaithful, they were not only themselves subject to judgment, but the nation as a whole suffered.[11]

The Hebrew prophets called Israel to live the Covenant faithfully, and denounced the abuse or ignorance of the Law not only in regard to their performance of explicit legal requirements (including those referring to offerings, tithes, etc.) but also to the spirit underlying the Law, and its concern for justice, particularly to the poor and oppressed. The judgment of God pronounced by the prophets was addressed to the leaders of Israel, and corporately to Israel as a whole. This communal aspect of justice meant that the prophetic indictments were not simply a condemnation of the individuals who may have been personally guilty of the offenses addressed, but directed to Israel as *a people*. Their corporate fidelity to the Covenant would be tested, and against them the wrathful judgment of God would be unleashed, if there was no repentant change in their behavior.[12]

The prophetic utterances of Isaiah are characteristic of the prophetic tradition in this regard:

'What are your endless sacrifices to me?' says Yahweh. 'I am sick of holocausts of rams and the fat of calves. The blood of bulls and of goats revolts me. When you come to present yourselves before me, who asked you to trample over my courts? Bring me your worthless offerings no more...

When you stretch out your hands I turn my eyes away. You may multiply your prayers, I shall not listen. Your hands are covered with blood. Wash, make yourselves clean. Take your wrong-doing out of my sight. Cease to do evil, learn to do good. Search for justice, help the oppressed, be just to the orphan, plead for the widow.'

(Is. 1: 11-13, 16-17)

Here, stewardship of the whole of life is emphasized, and the religious observances (as dictated in the Law) become a witness to the religious hypocrisy of Israel. Israel continues to make its offerings and sacrifices, but these are of no effect because there exists an inner disposition of the rebellion in the corporate soul of Israel, manifest in the daily acts of life, which is exemplified not only by failure to extend care for the poor, but even worse, the outright oppression of the poor. Here again, we see the *unworthy offering*. The prophets cry out for a renewal of the inner heart of Israel and a change of behavior. A similar sentiment is echoed in many of the other prophets (i.e. Amos 5:21-26, Jer. 6:16-20, Hos. 6:6). Whether the sin is idolatry or injustice, it must be remedied through repentance—the justice of God is not to be turned aside by a simple religious sacrifice.

One of the most illustrative passages about tithing is the complaint of the Lord against His people in Malachi 3:6-12. In this passage, the withholding of the tithe is likened to robbery, and seen as the cause for God's judgment. But a promise is given as well, for when the Lord's people, "bring the full tithes and dues", he promises to "open the floodgates of heaven and pour out blessings in abundance." (Mal. 3:11) For Israel, faithfulness to offering the tithe was one test of faithfulness to the Covenant. But this offering, as a religious symbol, needed to be an external (sacramental) sign of a total consecration of the inner life to God as well, as evidenced by acts of justice and mercy.

Stewardship in Israel as Manifest in the Writings

The dynamics of religious expression in Israel, particularly through worship in the Temple, give witness to the omnipresent influence of the

Law in the daily life of the Hebrews. The Psalms proclaim the joy of worship in the temple and manifest the inner thoughts of the Psalmist about the orientation of the heart toward God in worship, and the ordering of his material life as a result of that perspective.[13] The human heart and mind, directed rightly toward God, offers a sacrifice of praise and thanksgiving to Him (Ps. 115:13). A favorite in the Orthodox Church is Psalm 50(51), the great psalm of repentance of David.[14] In this psalm, the repentant David seeks, in faith, a cleansing of his heart and forgiveness of his sins. He commits himself to a restored life toward God and neighbor. The last several verses are of particular note:

> Sacrifice gives you no pleasure, were I to offer holocaust, you would not have it. My sacrifice is this broken spirit, you will not scorn this crushed and broken heart...
>
> Show your favor graciously to Zion, rebuild the walls of Jerusalem. Then there will be proper sacrifice to please you—holocausts and whole oblations - and young bulls to be offered on your altar.[15]

Ps.51:16-19

In this passage, the Psalmist longs to offer a righteous sacrifice to the Lord, but is unable to do so, because of his sin. However, because of his change of heart, his repentance becomes his sacrifice, and through repentance he is reconciled with God. When the heart has been restored through repentance, the person can again offer gifts in a religious, external context in righteousness.[16]

Wisdom literature often speaks of the practicalities of the management of money, always with a mind to virtuous and prudent exercise of its stewardship.[17] The themes of wise management, care for the poor, debts, honesty in monetary affairs, danger of the love of wealth, etc. all form part of the great 'backdrop' of the Judeo-Christian moral heritage about the matters of personal behavior regarding financial affairs.[18] Again these are always seen in their fullest context, a life lived before the face of God and in the midst of the community, which includes those who are poor.

Review of Hebrew Scriptures and Stewardship

From this brief overview, it is clear that the origins of many fundamental practices and beliefs regarding stewardship of material wealth in Christian thought originate in the Pentateuch; although some of these themes would be reinterpreted in light of the New Covenant.[19] However, the witness of the Hebrew Scriptures is not limited to the Pentateuch. The themes of offering, sacrifice and worship permeate the Prophetic and Wisdom literature as well, because offering and worship were cornerstones of the dictates of the Lord in the Covenant itself.

In reviewing these themes, several aspects consistently present themselves across the breadth of the Hebrew scripture. First and foremost, it is the Lord who is the source of all creation so that the cosmos is a manifestation of His goodness; human beings are entrusted as stewards of creation, created in the image and likeness of God. The Fall is the result of a proud failure by Adam to offer creation back to God in priestly thanksgiving. In the fallen world, sin is manifest through the misuse and abuse of creation by humans. The central act of religious, sacrificial offering is prompted by the heart, as well as commanded by God. Such offerings, when offered with an upright spirit, will lead to a joyous inner communion with God. God looks upon the heart of the one who offers and knows whether the offering is made in a righteous spirit, or if the disposition of the giver is in some way flawed. God's acceptance of the offering is determined according to this inner disposition, as manifested in relationship and fidelity to the Covenant, particularly in the treatment of those who are disadvantaged.

In establishing His Covenant with the Hebrews, the Lord set forth commandments regarding the right worship and stewardship of creation by humankind, including the manner of liturgical offerings and the construction of the Temple. The prophets gave witness to the judgment of God upon Israel whenever the stewardship of the gift of the Covenant itself was being ignored or abused. Orthodoxy interprets the first Covenant typologically, seeing in the offerings of Noah, Abraham, the Patriarchs, etc. a prefigurement of the perfect and acceptable offering by Jesus, the Messiah and High Priest.

PART I

The Practices of Stewardship in the Emergent Christian Church

Icon of the Encounter of Our Lord in the Temple
St. Sophia Seminary - South Bound Brook, NJ

CHAPTER THREE

NEW TESTAMENT STEWARDSHIP

Offering As a Sign of the New Covenant

Introduction to a New Testament Perspective on Stewardship

There is no shortage of New Testament material discussing the Christian attitude toward the offering of one's material means for godly purposes. From the numerous teachings of Christ in the Synoptic Gospels on wealth (and the danger therein), to the monetary collection promoted by the Apostle Paul on behalf of the suffering brothers and sisters of the Church of Jerusalem, the New Testament addresses these issues from a somewhat different perspective than the Old Testament.

If the premise - that the fundamental nature of human stewardship is to be found in sacrificial offering - is true, then the advent of the Messiah would signal a shift in the nature of stewardship to a new *theological* dynamic based upon the sacrificial offering of Christ. This Christocentric stewardship approach begins with the personal restoration of communion of human beings with God, through the Incarnation and the priestly sacrifice of the incarnate Christ revealed in the Paschal Mystery. Restored to a right relationship with the Lord and united to His Will in humility, humans are then able to exercise their sacred responsibilities as priestly stewards of their own lives and of other dimensions of creation which have been entrusted to them by God.

Accordingly, the Old Testament offerings prescribed by God have been supplanted by the priestly sacrifice of Christ and the Church. The traditional religious structures for offering in Hebrew society (including the Temple) would also be replaced in the New Testament Church.[1] New Testament writings attest to the distinctive shift in the pattern of participation in worship in the early Church, which moves from worship in the Temple to independent gatherings of Christians in house churches. This shift signals the emergence of a self-understanding wherein the Church sees Herself as the New Jerusalem, in communion with the Lord through the New Covenant, whose ongoing sacrificial offering was the Eucharistic. (Acts 2:46, 1Cor. 10). The Christian community would exemplify a vision of stewardship as *ministry* centered in the person of Christ, who was seen not only as the High Priest, but also the Gift that was offered and continues to be offered.[2] The New Testament also attests to a spiritual emphasis on a correct attitude toward earthly treasures, and its exercise in holy stewardship through Christian charity, in imitation of Christ.

To properly situate a discussion of stewardship in the New Testament, it might be helpful to briefly review the characteristics of the Hebrew faith community at the time of Christ and the influences of prominent religious groups on Hebrew thought and political leadership in light of the contemporary scholarship. In this era, Palestine was a confluence of many philosophical, political, religious and sociological streams. There was no wholly unified Hebrew religious mindset or understanding as such; rather a number of competing groups influenced not only religious thought, but also the very events of the New Testament. Some of these groups appear prominently in the Gospels; Jesus would speak to the Pharisees and the Sadducees directly about their beliefs and practices.[3] While background information about the beliefs and practices of these groups is somewhat scant or conflicting, it can be inferred that their influences on the teachings and practices of Second Temple Judaism and the New Testament church were significant.[4]

Another distinct group, the Essenes, may have been influential in the development of certain aspects of early Christian thought and practice.[5] For example, the Dead Sea scrolls attest to specific directives about the manner of offering sacrifices in the Temple, thus emphasizing the importance of sacrificial offering in the worship of

God.[6] Similarly, they placed a strong importance on community life, seeing the faith community as the new temple (Eph. 2:21). They also emphasized the importance of ritual washings (perhaps influencing early Christian baptism practices), as well as fasting and ascetic practices.[7]

The prominence of these groups in Hebrew society was related to their corporate socioeconomic status, and the clan-lineage of the people. Hence, the Sadducees, whose origins are believed to come from Zadok the high priest, would place a strong emphasis on cultic adherence at the temple and had many followers in the leadership of the Sanhedrin. The Pharisees are believed to have had a more popular appeal, emphasizing strong adherence to the practice of the Law in the everyday activities of life.[8] Paul, who was a Pharisee, schooled by Gamaliel (Acts 22:3), and as one with a certain authority in the Hebrew community, would have been knowledgeable of the teachings and inner workings of these not only of the Pharisees but also the polemics with the Sadducees, the Essenes and others.[9]

Contemporary commentators holding to the so-called 'New Perspectivist' view, would maintain that Second Temple Judaism (as present at the time of Christ) was a complex of competing religious forces.[10] In doing so, they challenge a commonly held view that the Pharisees at the time of Christ were simply blind adherents to a legalistic interpretation of the Law. They assert that the Protestant Reformers misunderstood the nature of Judaism in the biblical writings—seeing it as essentially legalistic. According to the New Perspective, this inadequate view of Judaism arose out of a polemic against excesses in Roman Catholic thought and practice at the time of the Reformation, but remains a powerful force in the contemporary Protestant view of the New Testament as a whole, and particularly Pauline writings.[11]

The issue is important for this discussion of stewardship because it raises the question of how the stewardship practices as embodied in Hebrew thought (and practice) are to relate to the stewardship *praxis* of the Church of the New Testament. For example, were the dictates of God embedded in Levitical teachings, such as the offering of first fruits and tithes, to become norms of Christian behavior as well?[12] The general applicability of the Law was of deep concern to the early Church, and the Council of Jerusalem (Acts 15: 6-29) set forth directives concerning the *praxis* of the Christian way. Hence, the Church would direct that circumcision was not to be required in the Christian community, while abstinence from spiritually harmful practices, (e.g. sexual immorality), was necessary. E. P. Sanders notes:

> The argument [against requiring circumcision] of Galatians is against Christian missionaries, not against Judaism, and it is against the view that Gentiles must accept the law as a condition of or as a basic requirement for membership. Paul's argument is not in favor of faith per se, nor is it against works per se. It is much more particular: it is against requiring the Gentiles to keep the Law of Moses in order to be true "sons of Abraham."[13]

In a Tradition-based Orthodox hermeneutic, the Old Covenant is perfected and surpassed by Jesus the Messiah, who fulfills the Law perfectly while initiating a New Covenant for a new people of God, who are initiated into the community through baptism, not circumcision. The "sons of Abraham" are the people of the New Covenant are called to walk by faith and fulfill the will of God in the Spirit of love, bestowed upon the New Jerusalem—the Church. Stewardship will be an important principle underlying the *praxis* of this new life by the Christian believers, as manifest in a sacrificial love of God and neighbor.

The Thanksgiving Offerings of Joseph and Mary— Luke 1, 2

The infancy narratives of Matthew and Luke not only serve as a narrative bridge between the Old and New Testaments, but also as an interpretive link between the practices and underlying beliefs of the Old Testament with those of the New Testament. Luke presents the stories of the angelic appearances to Zechariah and Mary in a manner that is completely harmonious with the context of Jewish worship and prophetic anticipation. Both Luke and Matthew identify Jesus, born of Mary, with the Messianic promises of the Old Testament. The structures of the thanksgiving prayers of both Zechariah and Mary are typical of this effort.[14] While they announce the grace of God in forms that are like psalms in structure, both hymns have a prophetic character as well, revealing that something new is being ushered forth by these events.

Mary, prompted by her Hebraic faith,[15] makes the traditional sacrificial offering of her first-born son who "opens the womb"[16] of two "turtledoves or pigeons," for this purpose.[17] This offering places a strong emphasis on God's love for the underprivileged - the poor are the favored by God, while the rich are endangered by their wealth. This theme is a favorite of Luke and creates a certain tension with those aspects of the Hebrew scripture which identified the favor of God with acquisition of wealth and fortune.[18] The *Magnificat* of Mary speaks of the Lord reversing the fortunes of the poor, the lowly, the hungry, etc. This theme will be echoed in Luke's version of the Beatitudes, which contrasts the blessed state of the lowly with the dangerous state of those who are wealthy, the satiated, and the comfortable.[19]

Mary's offering, however, is presented by Luke as more than a mere ritual. It is manifestation of the divine—through the prophetic utterances of both Simeon and Anna, who are present in the temple. The gifts of Mary are acceptable, for Mary bears not only the turtledoves, but also the Son whom she has borne.[20] This presentation of the Son by Mary prefigures the possibility of humankind (through the Incarnation) offering a perfect sacrifice in the person of the Messiah. This acceptable sacrifice will be fulfilled by Christ in the offering of Himself as the God-human on the cross.[21] The actions of Mary and Zechariah, true to their Hebraic faith, usher forth a new manifestation of the word of God acting in power, restoring the fortunes of the lowly and reclaiming the world for God.

The Parables of Christ on Stewardship

The Synoptic gospels are replete with parables and teachings about the right attitude and relationship that followers of Jesus are to have regarding money. Examples of these teachings include: the Teaching on Almsgiving (Mt. 6:1ff), Parable of the Hidden Treasure (Mt. 13:44-46), the Parable of the Rich Fool (Lk. 12:16-21), the encounter of the Rich Young Man (Mt. 19:16-30), etc.[22] Jesus spoke to many other topics affiliated with stewardship as well, such the importance of trust in God for provision of material things, care of the poor, and even paying taxes.

One of the clearest teachings on stewardship comes from the Parable of the Talents found in Mt. 25:14-30. The placement of this Gospel in the Matthean composition as one of the final teachings of Christ lends additional weight to the Church's understanding of the importance of this parable, referring as it does to the imminent departure (and return) of the Master. In this parable, the life of faith is likened to the execution of sound financial stewardship of certain substantial sums entrusted by the master to his servants. The return of the master after a long period of time may well be reflective of the early Church's understanding of issues raised by the delay in the *parousia*, and the importance of faithfulness to the master's directive to be good stewards of the gifts bestowed upon the early Church.[23] Those who are faithful stewards are rewarded, while judgment is pronounced on the wicked and lazy servant who buries his treasure; fear of the master is not an acceptable defense at the time of judgment.

The parable has exceptional importance for this discussion because of its explicit development of the stewardship theme, using terminology familiar to hearers at the time, (and also used elsewhere in the Gospel), to liken the spiritual stewardship of the Kingdom to the material stewardship with which all would be familiar.[24] Several aspects stand out. What is entrusted is a *treasure*. The description of the events uses financial terminology: talent (an exceeding large sum of money), bankers, interest, etc. The treasure is entrusted to humans, who will be responsible not only for its preservation, but also, to a degree, its rightful increase. The sound management of earthly gifts proves the worthiness to rule over more.[25]

It should also be noted that the one thing that defeats the unworthy steward was *fear*. Again it is the inner orientation which draws our focus, in this case where fidelity of relationship with the Master and obedience as a servant is subverted by fear in the heart of the servant, prompting him to faithless, foolish, and unworthy behavior. For the follower of Christ, the fidelity to the Master is to be based in trust, or faith, and manifest in action. This faith is affirmed by the belief in His return and the need to give an account for his stewardship.

The Orthodox interpretation of this parable has often extended beyond the stewardship of earthly things, to also include the stewardship of spiritual matters. St. Gregory the Great notes that,

> "The Lord who dispensed the talents returns to demand an account, because He who now generously bestows spiritual gifts may at the judgment inquire searchingly into what was achieved; He may take into account what everyone has received and weigh up the gain we bring back from His gifts."[26]

The earthly stewardship of material goods serves as a *template* for the exercise of the stewardship of spiritual gifts. Stewardship of spiritual and material gifts is to be exercised from the perspective of the inevitability of the Master's return and the requirement to give an account to the Master. In the end, all is returned to the Master, who is the true Lord of all things, spiritual and material, and of all people. The theme of joy is conspicuous as well, paralleling other expressions in the stewardship narratives found in both the Old and New Testaments. Those who are faithful are invited to enter into nothing less than the joy of the Master.

While the parable stands on its own, the connection to the prophecy of the Last Judgment (Mt. 25:31-46) that follows provides useful context as well. The stewardship of Christian life (time, talent, treasure) must be characterized by an inner spirit of charity toward the least of the brethren. The reward for such faithful stewardship, exemplified by love of neighbor, is the joy of the kingdom, while the failure to offer charity results in eternal judgment and condemnation. The stakes regarding the exercise of human stewardship are quite high.

The Widow's Mite (Mk. 12:40- 44, Lk. 21:1-4)

This encounter speaks most eloquently to the nature of sacred offerings and the importance of the *intent in the heart* of the one who offers. In Mark, this story is situated so as to contrast the widow's witness to selfless generosity against the behavior of the Pharisees, who are rebuked for their pride and the devouring of the savings of widows. Similarly, the spiritual character of the widow's offering is juxtaposed to apostles' fixation on the material beauty of the restored Temple, prompting the prophetic warning of Christ about its forthcoming destruction (Mk. 13:1-4).[27] This context is important, for the Pharisees and the apostles both considered the notion of offerings in the temple as important (as did Jesus), but their blindness to the importance of the generosity in the widow's soul prompt the commentary of Christ about such things.

The widow's offering was an offering of totality (v. 44) that far exceeded the notion of the first fruits offering or percentage (as in a tithe). Christ would ridicule the Pharisees and scribes on this very point (Mt. 23.23f), in their rigid observance of the external tithe, but lacking the inner spirit of mercy, generosity and true justice exemplified by the widow.[28] *Total consecration of the soul* in giving is key to the New Testament Christian view of stewardship for it mirrors the attitude of Christ himself, who offered Himself, in condescending to take flesh and suffer death, even "death on a cross."[29] Hence, the actual offering (surrender) of the coins is important, as a visible symbol of the inner disposition of the soul.[30] There is also an inherent message about trust of God, reminiscent of the teaching in Matthew (Ch.5); God is the One who will supply all material things of earthly life, especially for the one who has given over all to Him.

Warnings of Jesus against Avarice

While space does not allow a discussion of many of the other teachings of Christ regarding stewardship, for example the stewardship implications of the parable of the Good Samaritan,

Christ frequently warned against avarice (e.g. Lk. 16:13, Mt. 19:23-25). Indeed, avarice is often seen as the motivation of Judas Iscariot to betray Christ.[31] In a final, bittersweet 'offering', Judas offers his ill-gotten spoils, the thirty pieces of silver for betraying Christ, by casting them into the temple. And, as in the case with Cain, the sin of avarice and the failure to offer a righteous sacrifice leads to despondency and murder—in this case the murder of the Messiah and the suicide of Judas.

Acts of the Apostles—the Offerings of the Early New Testament Community

The portrait of life in the New Testament Church, while sometimes romanticized, nevertheless reveals an emerging apostolic Christian community coming to grips with sharing a communal life in the Spirit. Men and women, rich and poor, were drawn into the Christian fellowship in ways that must certainly have upset existing social mores. The later inclusion of the Gentiles must have posed even greater challenges. Characteristic of this early community was a call to offer and share one's personal goods with the community.

One of the most vivid (and chronologically important) portraits is that of the offering of Ananias and Sapphira (Acts 5:1-11), who sell a piece of property and present some of the proceeds to the apostles. In what must have been a visible display of vanity and deceit, they withheld some of the proceeds of the sale. The apostle Peter, inspired so as to know the truth of the deception, pronounces the judgment of God upon their hidden sin. The givers are struck dead when their sin is exposed. In some ways, this recalls the unacceptable offering of Cain, where there is an interior withholding in the process of offering, rather than a free and loving surrender of all. The offering of Ananias and Sapphira is tainted by the inner attitude of the heart, and the judgment of the deception is harsh and swift, bringing a sense of holy fear in the midst the whole church in that day.

The words of St. Peter illuminate the seriousness of the sin and the Christian understanding of why this seemingly 'small' sin was punished so harshly. Peter's words to Ananias (and later Sapphira) describe this offering as nothing less than a lie against the Holy Spirit.[32] Peter is inspired to realize that Ananias has not opened his heart to God in submission, but rather has been led by the Satan - the Father of Lies - to try to deceive even God Himself. Later, when Sapphira would be asked about the sum received for the land, she would lie when confronted directly about the amount of her offering, refusing to acknowledge the deception in her soul. Her punishment is equally swift. Jesus Himself had challenged the Pharisees on this very issue—the external manifestation of adherence to the Law and spiritual things while the inner heart was utterly at odds with the Spirit of truth and true charity. Offerings are to be made in transparent humility before God and the Church; this requires a self emptying and submission to God rather than self-justification.

It is also clear that offerings were now being made to the new ministers of the Church, the apostles. Luke reports that, "All who owned property or houses sold them and donated the proceeds. They used to lay them at the feet of the apostles to be distributed to everyone according to his need." (Acts 4:34) The narrative continues, describing the acceptable offering of one Joseph of Cyprus, who received the name Barnabas or 'Son of Encouragement.' There is a connection here to the encouragement of the community when presented with such a gift. The full effect of the fraud of Ananias and Sapphira can best be understood in this contrast.[33]

The pericope also introduces a key element in the life of the early Church - the communal life of charitable care for the poor and needy, particularly widows and orphans. The offerings were meant to improve the lot of those who lacked these material goods. This theme will be repeated throughout the New Testament, and indeed throughout Christian history, becoming a sign of the authenticity of the Christian message—the Church practices what it preaches. This may be another reason why the judgment of the deceit and fraud of Ananias and Sapphira was so severe, in that it jeopardized the dynamic witness of the Church and the apostles as well as its integrity. Clearly these demonstrations of offering were public, and the community gained strength and encouragement through the visible sacrifice of others.[34] The entry of a spirit of deception and discouragement cast a pall over the community and presented a grave danger to the integrity of its witness.

One aspect of the story needs further review - the teaching of Peter embedded in the rebuke of Ananias - which sheds light on the manner of giving in the early Church. He says, "Was it not yours so long as it remained unsold? Even when you sold it, was not the money still yours?" (Acts 5:4f.) In so speaking, Peter makes the point that there was no compulsion to make the offering. The offering was not a precondition to participation in the community. What was important was the inner attitude, identifying the character and quality of the gift. In this case, the gift of Ananias and Sapphira, while substantial, was marred by their inner disposition. Their offering can be contrasted to the spirit of true, abundant generosity offered in freedom, as exemplified by Barnabas, and the power of such gifts to lift the community in encouragement.

It is also important to note the priestly and prophetic role of Peter, who receives the gifts on behalf of the community and the Lord. He directs the further administration of the gifts offered for the care of the community.[35] A pattern of sacred order in the Church emerges within a type of 'service' of receiving (and distributing) the offering may be implied, although there is no evidence of a formal ritual as such. The ordering of the ministry of these gifts would be further exemplified by the call and ordination of the seven deacons (Acts 6) and the spiritual self-offering of the Protomartyr Stephen.

There are several other passages in Acts where the preaching of the Gospel brings financial hardship on people who make a living from paganism. Hence, Paul's preaching prompts a riot led by Demetrius the silversmith, who astutely recognizes that the success of the Paul will hurt his the trade in silver idols. (Acts 20:23ff.) A similar outcome occurs when Paul heals the girl with the clairvoyant spirit who made money for her handlers by predicting fortunes (Acts 16:16ff). These men have Paul imprisoned when their source of income is ruined after he delivers the girl from the demon's power. Such stories highlight the transience of worldly treasures when juxtaposed to the eternal gift of spiritual healing as manifest by the dynamic action of the Church. The advent of the Gospel challenges the financial status quo in the world.

The Collection of Paul on Behalf of the Church of Jerusalem[36]

The apostle Paul was one of the great preachers of stewardship in the New Testament. In his letters, Paul repeatedly appealed to the churches he had established on his missionary journeys to support those in need, particularly the brethren in the Church of Jerusalem during the time of acute famine. In his analysis of the inner motivation for such giving, Paul emphasizes liberality and generosity. He connects the conversion of the churches of Macedonia to their material offering - "…[T]hey offered their own selves first to God and, under God, to us.[37]" (2 Cor.8:5) Their charitable giving was a fruit of their inner conversion to Christ as well as an outward display of it. Paul parallels the Corinthian Church's riches and favor[38] received from Christ to the invitation to charity and self-emptying, saying, "Remember how generous the Lord Jesus was: he was rich, but became poor for your sake, to make you rich out of his poverty."[39] Such gifts have both a material and spiritual character; human generosity makes the grace of God visible in the Church. It is important to note that Paul, while exhorting the faithful to finish the task of the collection campaign, also instructs them not to utterly impoverish themselves in doing so, saying,

> This does not mean that to give relief to others you ought to make things difficult for yourselves: it is a question of balancing what happens to be your surplus now against their present need, and one day they may have something to spare that will supply your own need. This is how we strike a balance; as scripture says: The man who gathered much had none too much; the man who gathered little did not go short.

> *2 Cor.9:13-15*

The goal is a communal equality and sharing, not an overt magnanimity (vainglory) that loses sight of this communal view of sharing the blessings of God in joy. The self-emptying described above means submitting one's personal or individualistic needs or desires to serve the greater needs of both the local and distant Church communities.

Furthermore, while being concerned about the inner disposition of the givers (exhorting them to do so in cheerfulness); Paul reports that the administration of the gifts to the recipients in the Church is cause for much gratitude and praise of God.[40] They are to rejoice in the confession of their brethren as demonstrated by the liberality of their giving as a sign of 'fellowship.'[41] The gifts are the result of true generosity—Paul sends Titus and two of the brethren to assure that the gift is ready and that they are not the result of extortion (9:5). The result of this offering is a spirit of gratitude and the encouragement to zeal for the faithful (9:3). The offering of the gifts is proof of the charity residing in their hearts (8:24).

These verses imply a liturgical context for celebrating and participating in the saving, indescribable gift of God.[42] Paul calls the offering a "holy service" prompting "thanksgiving to God."[43] By making such offerings, human beings participate in the work of Christ in love by emptying of self in the human realm, as exemplified by offering from one's material means to the apostle, the minister of the Church, who will see to it that it is rightly used to God's purposes. The Corinthian community, through charity, works synergistically with the apostolic ministers, who are their link to the fellowship of the broader Church. It is clear that this offering accomplishes far more than pragmatically providing a measure of material assistance to those in need.[44] Rather, the offering becomes a manifestation of the charity and generosity of God Himself and the work of the Spirit of charity in the Church.

Hebrews—Theology of the Righteous Sacrifice

While much can be said about the liturgical theology and imagery in the Epistle to the Hebrews concerning the New Testament view of the nature of sacrifice, most of the epistle refers specifically to that which is accomplished by the sacrifice of Christ as a fulfillment and perfection of that which took place in the first Covenant.[45] The author of Hebrews contrasts the perfect offering of Christ on the cross with the offering of the Old Testament gifts and sacrifices as prescribed by the Law.[46] The latter are seen as ineffective in restoring humanity to communion with God, being incapable of "bringing worshippers to perfection" (10:1). Hence, sacrifices based on the Law needed to be offered again and again. However, the offering of Christ (the High Priest) of His own body once and for all, does accomplish and fulfill the sacrificial imperative of humanity in relationship with God perfectly. His sacrifice is a totally sufficient offering for sin and effects the restoration of the relationship of humanity with the God in Himself (10:12).

However, if the people of the New Covenant are to be faithful to that covenant, they must attend to the exhortation, "Do not neglect good deeds and generosity: God is pleased by sacrifices of this kind." (13:16) It is clear from this that sacrificial acts by Christians are not abolished in the New Testament; rather, they are reinterpreted in the light of the sacrificial offering of Christ and joined to that offering.[47] The exhortation to do good works links the human endeavor of personal charity with the sacrificial offering of Christ Himself, and the divine mandate of love of neighbor, accomplishing the perfection of the saints.

The Johannine Tradition: Support for Missionary Work of the Church (3 Jn. 5-8)

In this short epistle, the 'Elder', commends Gaius and his community on extending hospitality toward the Elder's fellow disciples, who are engaged as itinerant evangelists working in Asia Minor.[48] Not only is this example of charity referred to as "faithful work," but also as a duty; the passage concludes that it is "...our responsibility to welcome men of this sort and contribute our share to their work for the truth." (v.8)

By this late date, it is evident that the Church fully supported ministers of the gospel in the work of propagation of the Gospel.[49] In fact, the faithful are encouraged to be supportive precisely because the apostolic effort is not supported by the non-believers, but by the Church. In supporting these missionaries financially, the faithful share in their work in the proclamation of the name of Christ. What is evolving at this point is a mechanism of stewardship as financial offering so as to support the missionary work of the Church. The work of these missionaries might be likened to the Levites, who had to rely on the support of the community for their livelihood. The charity of the faithful disciples is contrasted to the leadership of the local community, exemplified by Diotrophes, who has not accepted the apostolic witness of missionaries who act in the name of the elder/apostle.[50] In this example, it is also clear that the spirituality of one's faith relationship with Christ is to be exemplified by believers through their charity to the Church, in this case embodied by supporting the missionaries in their midst.

The Priestly Offering of Christ in the Gospel of John

The high theological style and design of the Gospel according to St. John, when compared to the Synoptic gospels, places a secondary importance on the explicit stewardship of material goods. Nevertheless, the liturgical style of this Gospel enhances the basis for the Orthodox Church's liturgical-theological understanding of the New Testament and the fulfillment of the sacrifice by Christ—the Lamb of God - for the life of the world. The narrative of the Gospel reveals layers of teaching in the Final Discourses in Jn. 13-16, which climax in the 'High Priestly' prayer of Christ in John 17. Here Christ prays to the Father, lifting up the apostolic community to the Father and commending the disciples and their work after the Resurrection to the Father. Through His glorification on the cross, Christ invokes a priestly consecration on the Church—making the disciples holy, as well as all those who are to come to believe in Him through their ministry.

The content of this prayer as placed in the arrangement of John's gospel reveals the consecratory dimension of human stewardship.[51] This consecratory action of the new High Priest is to bring about a new communion of God and humanity. The Orthodox Church focuses on this higher sense of stewardship as transcending merely utilitarian or material ends; rather, the offering of earthly gifts prefigures the quintessentially spiritual, priestly offering of Christ on the cross and His glorification.[52]

After the resurrection (Jn. 21), Christ would appear to Peter and several other apostles along the shore of Tiberius, perform the miracle of the draught of fishes, and share with them a meal with Eucharistic symbolism. In light of this encounter, the disciples are made to realize their mission of consecration of the world and their own priestly ministry. They are to begin the work to which they were consecrated by Christ's High Priestly prayer in Jn. 17. This passage also describes this ministry in terms of the shepherding of the sheep. The apostles are called to be 'good shepherds', like Christ who is 'The Good Shepherd' (John 10) who has laid down his life for the flock. Such is the stewardship of souls exercised by the Church. Stewardship in the Church is no longer limited to the material world, but a call to share in the exercise of salvific priestly spiritual work of Christ in the world, for the life of the world. It may be supposed that the late date of this Gospel makes this understanding part of the great legacy of the apostles to the Church - this understanding of spiritual stewardship in the continuing apostolic ministry of the Church.[53] In the view of Orthodox anthropology, this is the true restoration of humankind to its original priestly dignity, and more, as a fruit of the Incarnation and Paschal Mystery.

Summary of the Biblical Witness

The theme of stewardship is highly developed in both the Old and New Testaments. In Genesis, the blueprint for an Orthodox anthropology is sketched in the creation narratives. The fundamental nature of man as one who offers the first fruits of creation is illustrated by the juxtaposition of the acceptable sacrifice of Abel, and the effects of sin manifest in the unworthy sacrifice of Cain. The mysterious encounter of Abram with Melchizedek and the offering of the tithe to this priest and king is a key Old Testament type of the sacrificial priestly work of Christ, and the invitation to others to share in the priestly work through the offering of material tithes and sacrifices. Tithes would eventually become the basic unit of material stewardship, but they also had a deeper representative meaning as a sign of the participation in thanksgiving in the Covenant of the Chosen People. Tithes were to be offered in the spirit of thanksgiving, not from compulsion, vainglory or covetousness while providing a practical means of supporting the Levitical ministers, as God willed.

In the New Testament, the Infancy Narratives serve as a transition between the Old and New Testaments - revealing the faithfulness of Mary and Zechariah to the cult of Hebraic sacrifice while proclaiming a new vision thereof, and a coming New Covenant. Christ taught extensively on the right use of money and stewardship, decrying the legalism of the Pharisaic attitudes toward the tithes and commending generosity and care for the poor, exemplified by the offering of widow in the temple.[54]

The practices of stewardship in the apostolic church appear very early in Acts of the Apostles, where there is a juxtaposition of the acceptable offering of the land of Barnabas and the unacceptable offering of Ananias and Sapphira. Offerings were often used for the local church, to meet the needs of the poor, especially widows and orphans and a symbol of the common life together. The collection by the apostle Paul on behalf of the Church of Jerusalem, and the encouragement by the apostolic Elder in the Johannine tradition to support missionaries in Asia Minor, gives evidence to a growing awareness of a global mission of stewardship of material wealth by the Church for the furtherance of the Gospel and support of the Church. The spiritual development of the theme of stewardship would reach a summit in the Gospel of St. John, in the High Priestly prayer of Christ and its fulfillment in the glorification of Christ on the Cross, and the Church's mission as stewards/shepherds/priests who exercise spiritual stewardship of souls.

In these passages a number of recurring themes appear, which will serve as points of reference in upcoming chapters:

- the offering of first fruits/tithes,

- acceptable and unacceptable offerings,

- the importance of the freedom and generosity as proper interior attitudes,

- spiritual danger of the love of money

- centrality of thanksgiving (Eucharist) and joy, and

- the communal care of those in need and support of missionary work through stewardship funds.

- Christocentric vision of life in sacrificial imitation of the Lord

The next section will investigate the growth over two millennia of the Church's understanding of material and spiritual offerings, viewed from this biblical framework, in a multiplicity of contexts which have prompted both expression and evolution of the Church's teaching in regard to stewardship.

CHAPTER FOUR

STEWARDSHIP AS OFFERING IN ORTHODOX CHURCH HISTORY

Church Practice in Light of Church History

While the writings of the Bible illuminate the teaching and practices of Christ and the early Church, for the Orthodox it is not sufficient merely to recall the theoretical spiritual underpinnings of the Bible and early Church practice and assume that these have been and always will be the actual operative norms in Orthodox communities.[1] To the contrary, in American Orthodoxy today, offering practices have emerged which reflect a variety of theoretical and practical approaches, some of which may (or may not) be consistent with the ancient biblical models or subsequent Orthodox Tradition. This exploration of the historical evolution of Christian stewardship practices will chart the emergence of some of these patterns and their theoretical effect on parish life in twenty-first century Christinaity in America. Using the ancient, authentically Orthodox modes of stewardship (from both the Bible and Orthodox Tradition) will, hopefully, lead us to consider ways to apply these principles to contemporary Orthodox life.

Stewardship as *Oikonomia* in Orthodox History

Orthodoxy views 'stewardship' in terms of the Greek term 'oikonomia'—which can be loosely defined to mean: *a mode of responsible servanthood by one who is lesser, in service of one who is greater.*[2] The term, *oikonomos* (steward, house manager) with variants, appears frequently in the New Testament, particularly in parables where Jesus describes the 'servant' (disciple) as an *oikonomos*.[3] Orthodoxy also relates the term of *oikonomia* to that of *episkopos*—overseer, bishop, who is responsible for the oversight of the household of God. (Acts 20:28, Titus 1.7, 1Tim.3).[4] In this case the household is not merely a physical-material one, but the household of God, the Church. In Orthodoxy, the term *oikonomia*[5] was never seen as strictly a matter of pragmatic management of personal or corporate financial affairs, but rather referred more broadly to the whole of human life and the manner in which Christian life is to be lived, the spiritual dimension being preeminent.[6] As each Christian is to be a responsible steward, the bishop has the vocation to be chief steward of the local Church.[7] There was no sense of a separate 'theology of stewardship' in Orthodoxy, any more than there was a 'theology of ethics' or a 'theology of spirituality', rather Orthodoxy always focused on the multidimensional aspects of Christian life as a whole, of which what we call stewardship was an integral part.

Among the spiritual principles that characterize the practice of Orthodox stewardship over time, four are particularly noteworthy. Each of these aspects has evolved significantly in various times and places, yet each remains an important touchstone for an Orthodox understanding of stewardship and financial management. Because it is difficult to track these theoretical practices over time and in various cultures, this writing will focus primarily on stewardship as it is manifest in financial giving, with the caveat that a true understanding of Christian stewardship embraces the entire human person and institutional behaviors.

Offerings as a Basis for Stewardship

Across Christian traditions, monetary offerings made in the context of worship settings are a universal practice—however, the evolution of the underlying link between liturgical worship and offering is particularly rich in when viewed the lens of Orthodox liturgical sacrifice. The offering of gifts[8] is connected to the sacerdotal priesthood and liturgical worship of the Orthodox Church in the Eucharistic Liturgy, the sacred offering of the Body and Blood of Christ, the

High Priest.[9]   However, while the Divine Liturgy is a profoundly mystical and spiritual event, the material offerings of the faithful *are* inherently *linked* to this spiritual offering. By linking the offering of material gifts to the liturgical worship of God, the worshipper is led to see his offering as an offering to God, and not just to the Church as an isolated local institution, as if somehow separate from God. This distinction is important because it can become quite possible to orient giving practices to all manner of church related activities—giving to the Church institution in a way that fails to understand that the offerings are to be made, first and foremost, *to God*.

Tithes and Offerings in the Early Church

While a detailed examination of the question of the mode of making material offerings (or tithing) in the early church cannot be fully developed here it is important to note that the application of biblical teachings from sources dating to the end of the apostolic era and throughout the emerging patristic age.[10]   As the Church moved away from its Jewish moorings in the first century, most of the practices of the Law were either abrogated or reinterpreted in the Christian community. After the destruction of the temple, the practice of temple offerings became impossible. However, offerings were intrinsic to the Christian *ethos*, most clearly manifest in the Eucharistic assembly.

This essential link of the material offerings of the faithful to the Eucharistic offering of the Church community is clearly evident in a number of the earliest Christian writings. The *Didache* describes this offering in the following terms:

> Every first-fruit, therefore, of the products of wine-press and threshing-floor, of oxen and of sheep, you shall take and give to the prophets, for they are your high priests. But if you have not a prophet, give it to the poor. If you make a batch of dough, take the first-fruit and give according to the commandment. So also when you open a jar of wine or of oil, take the first-fruit and give it to the prophets; and of money (silver) and clothing and every possession, take the first-fruit, as it may seem good to you, and give according to the commandment.

> But every Lord's day gather yourselves together, and break bread, and give thanksgiving after having confessed your transgressions, that your sacrifice may be pure. But let no one that is at variance with his fellow come together with you, until they be reconciled, that your sacrifice may not be profaned. For this is that which was spoken by the Lord: In every place and time offer to me a pure sacrifice; for I am a great King, says the Lord, and my name is wonderful among the nations.[11]

This passage describe the offering of the first fruits of the people in the form of the 'batch of dough', and the 'wine' and 'oil' presented to the prophets - who were the primary celebrants of the Eucharistic worship of the Church community in this first century context. This activity was consistent with the key moral obligation of care for the neighbor in need, as reported earlier in the text. Note also that the celebrants of the Eucharistic liturgy were the recipients of the first fruits offering - ostensibly for their ministry and care (as in the case of the Levites) and for distribution to those in need

Similarly, the action of offering by the believers, in the context of the Eucharist, is a means to the alleviation of the needs of the poor, as is reported by Justin Martyr:

> When our prayer is ended, bread and wine and water are brought, and the president in like manner offers prayers and thanksgivings, according to his ability, and the people assent, saying 'Amen;' and there is a distribution to each, and a participation of that over which thanks have been given, and to those who are absent a portion is sent by the deacons. And they who are well-to-do, and willing, give what each thinks fit; and what is collected is deposited with the president, who succors the orphans and widows, and those who, through sickness or any other cause, are in want, and those who are in bonds, and the strangers sojourning among us, and in a word takes care of all who are in need.[12]

Here, there was no compulsion to give a *mandatory* gift or requirement to offer a percentage of one's wealth. The offerings were brought into a unity, and the Eucharistic liturgy, as celebrated by the president (bishop or perhaps the prophet) who also then serves as overseer of the distribution of the offerings of the material gifts on behalf of those in need within the community, and beyond. That these earliest sources note the practice of offering and the offering of material gifts denotes an internal understanding of their importance and meaning - hence these practices are reported, in some detail. These are given as instructions, perhaps in part because the communities were not always consistent in their practices.

The following passage, also from St. Justin, explains the interrelationship of the spiritual offering of first fruits with the Christian understanding of spiritual, Eucharistic offerings and their material counterpart (charity).

> The oblation of the Church, therefore, which the Lord gave instructions to be offered throughout all the world, is accounted with God a pure sacrifice, and is acceptable to Him; not that He stands in need of a sacrifice from us, but that he who offers is himself glorified in what he does offer, if his gift be accepted. For by the gift both honor and affection are shown forth towards the King; and the Lord, wishing us to offer it in all simplicity and innocence, did express Himself thus: "Therefore, when thou offerest thy gift upon the altar, and shalt remember that thy brother hath ought against thee, leave thy gift before the altar, and go thy way; first be reconciled to thy brother, and then return and offer thy gift." We are bound, therefore, to offer to God the first-fruits of His creation, as Moses also says, "Thou shalt not appear in the presence of the Lord thy God empty [handed];" so that man, being accounted as grateful, by those things in which he has shown his gratitude, may receive that honor which flows [there] from.
>
> And the class of oblations in general has not been set aside; for there were both oblations there [among the Jews], and there are oblations here [among the Christians]. Sacrifices there were among the people; sacrifices there are, too, in the Church: but the species alone has been changed, inasmuch as the offering is now made, not by slaves, but by freemen.

> For the Lord is [ever] one and the same; but the character
> of a servile oblation is peculiar [to itself], as is also that of
> freemen, in order that, by the very oblations, the indication
> of liberty may be set forth. For with Him there is nothing
> purposeless, nor without signification, nor without design.
> And for this reason they (the Jews) had indeed the tithes of
> their goods consecrated to Him, but those who have received
> liberty set aside all their possessions for the Lord's purposes,
> bestowing joyfully and freely not the less valuable portions
> of their property, since they have the hope of better things
> [hereafter]; as that poor widow acted who cast all her living
> into the treasury of God.[13]

Here, St. Justin notes how the Christian offering, as directed by
Jesus the Lord, supersedes that of Judaism and fulfills it spiritually.
It is a norm of the offering of *firstfruits* in both a material and
spiritual way. In writings of the post-apostolic period, a percentage
(tithe) does find mention in certain Church authorities, i.e. Cyprian
of Carthage.[14] By the fifth century, the practice of offering a tithe is
mentioned more clearly as a *type* of minimal offering, as juxtaposed to
the offering of 'everything', exemplified by the teachings of Christ. St.
Jerome put it this way:

> What we have said of tithes and first-fruits, which of old
> used to be given by the people to the priests and Levites,
> understand also in the case of the people of the church, to
> whom it has been commanded to sell all they have and give
> to the poor and follow the Lord. If we are unwilling to do
> this, at least let us imitate the rudimentary teaching of the
> Jews so as to give a part of the whole to the poor, and pay the
> priests and Levites due honor. If anyone shall not do this he is
> convicted of defrauding and cheating God.[15]

Similarly, St. John Cassian reflects the offering dynamics of his
day (late fourth century) when describing a young, married man's
extraordinary zeal to follow Christ—eventually renouncing the
world and becoming a monk, taking the name of Theonas.[16] As
a lay person, Theonas came to Abbot John with a group of others,

presenting his offerings—both spiritual and material—giving to the abbot them as "tithes and first fruits".[17] Abbot John graciously accepts the offerings of Theonas and the others saying,

> I am indeed delighted, my children, with the duteous liberality of your gifts; and your devout offering, the disposal of which is entrusted to me, I gratefully accept, because you are offering your firstfruits and tithes for the good and use of the needy, as a sacrifice to the Lord, of a sweet smelling savour, in the belief that by your offering of them, the abundance of your fruits and all your substance, from which you have taken away these for the Lord, will be richly blessed, and that you yourselves will, according to the faith of His command, be endowed even in this world with manifold richness in all good things…"[18]

However, Abbot John exhorts Theonas to go beyond the legal prescription of the Old Testament tithe:

> "For the righteous, for whom the law is not enacted, are thus shown to be not under the law, as they try not only to fulfill, but even to exceed the righteousness of the law, and their devotion is greater than the legal requirement, as it goes beyond the observance of precepts and adds to what is due of its own free will."[19]

Abbot John then explains how Abraham, David and other saints of the Old Testament went beyond the Law in their actions, "… as all of them were not satisfied with merely offering tithes of their possessions, but actually refused property, and offered them rather to God, themselves and their souls…"[20] He also reveals how the failure to offer a tithe is a sign of spiritual weakness,

> "And so if even those who, faithfully offering tithes of their fruits are obedient to the more ancient precepts of the Lord, cannot yet climb the heights of the gospel, you can see clearly how short of it those fall who do not even do this [the requirements of the old Law]. For how can those men

be partakers of the grace of the gospel who disregard the fulfillment even of the lighter command of the law, to the easy character of which the weighty words of the Giver of the law bear testimony as a curse is actually invoked on those who do not fulfill them . . ."[21]

Once again, Abbot John would differentiate the Christian way by emphasizing the *freedom* of the Christian to embrace the divine invitation to generosity offered by Christ, contrasting it to the Law which is executed by dictate,

"Here the grandeur of [the] sublime command [of Christ] is shown by the very fact that He does not *order*, but *exhorts*, saying: 'if thou wilt be perfect, go' and do this or do that. Here Moses lays a burden that cannot be refused on those who are unwilling: here Paul meets with counsels those who are willing and eager for perfection… Christ therefore does not constrain anyone, by the compulsion of a command, to those lofty heights of goodness, but stimulates them by the power of free will, and urges them on by wise counsels and the desire to perfection."[22]

He exhorts his hearers to go beyond the Law, in light of the New Testament, to the realm of grace and freely-willed generosity. In doing so, he emphasizes that this next step, beyond the minimum requirements, is a movement of the free will of the soul. Theonas' response is profound,

"…[H]e was greatly humiliated and conscience stricken because the old man had said not only that he had failed to attain to the perfection of the gospel, but also that he had scarcely fulfilled the commands of the law, since though he was accustomed every year to pay the tithes of his fruits as alms, yet he mourned that he had never even heard of the law of the firstfruits; and even if he had in the same way fulfilled this, he humbly confessed that still he would in the old man's eyes have been very far from the perfection of the Gospel."[23]

The story describes the Theonas' return to his wife, who adamantly refuses, because of her youth and desire for a life in the world, to respond to his entreaties to abandon the world. Eventually Theonas would leave her, so as to deprive himself of worldly goods to follow Christ and seek spiritual perfection.[24]

From this story we can clearly see a practice of offering tithes (or first fruits) in place in the fourth century Church of Palestine. However, it is also clear that tithing is not considered a norm of the Gospel *per se*, rather it is a beneficial practice, set in place by the Lord as with the rest of the Law, which the Christian is challenged to exceed through more abundant generosity and emptying of self. It is also interesting that the *monasteries* had become the places where the tithes and first fruits were offered, instead of the local *ecclesia* in the city.[25] This may have been a local phenomenon in Palestine and Egypt, yet it is clear that laity would support of the monasteries financially, not only as a charitable act toward the monastics themselves but also in support for the monastics' work in care of the poor. The shift from the offering-charitable work from the local church to the monasteries would, in some ways, become almost normative in Orthodoxy in both the Mediterranean, Slavic regions and the West - and is not without its problems.

Martyrdom - The First Fruits of the Resurrection

If the Mystery of Holy Baptism served as the initial consecration of one's life as an offering to Christ and a sharing in His offering of Himself unto His saving Death and Resurrection, then the realization of the implications of that consecration had profound effects upon the mindset of adherents to the Christian faith - fostering a desire to consecrate one's life to Christ. This was first realized, most perfectly, through the imitation of the holy martyrs - beginning with St. Stephen and the example of the holy apostles and their successors such as St. Ignatius of Antioch. This sense of offering emphasizes the Orthodox notion of the total consecration of one's life to God and martyrdom was a sign of the Kingdom realized in the sacrificial. life of the martyr in imitation of Christ's sacrificial death. While references to this language in the lives of the martyrs is common in the writings of the early Church, the martyrdom of St. Victor serves an example of this terminology,

> "The Saint suffered this mutilation with great joy, offering to God these first-fruits of his body. His barbaric tormentor condemned him to be put under the grindstone of a hand-mill and crushed to death."[26]

As exemplified in Byzantine liturgical poetry, the Kontakion of St. Romanos the Melodist to the Holy Martyrs summarized the belief and sentiment of the Church concerning the sacrifice of the martyr:

> *O Lord, The world offers to You, as the Father of creation,*
> *The God-bearing Martyrs as the first-fruits of nature.*
> *By their prayers through the Theotokos,*
> *Keep Thy Church in perfect peace, O Most Merciful One.*

This passage is sung on certain feasts of the martyrs, and embedded in the cyclic liturgy of the Church, notably on the First Sunday After Pentecost which is dedicated as the Sunday of All Saints in the Eastern Orthodox liturgical calendar. In Orthodoxy, the hymns of the Church reflect her internal understanding of the spiritual nature of human activity and the consecration of the soul to God.

These elements of Eucharistic worship, scriptural fulfillment, the totality of offering in martyrdom and the firstfruits of eternity frequently appear side by side in the catacombs, which served not only as burial grounds for the Christians (notably the martyrs) but also a place of liturgical remembrance and Eucharistic communion. The symbolism extent on the walls of the catacombs are replete with the imagery of biblical / Eucharistic meaning (loaves, fish, wine, bread, etc.) the lives of the martyrs, and the conjoined adherence of their followers to a similar consecration.

The Witness of Church Architecture Regarding Liturgical Offerings

One of the earliest known Christian churches is the house church of Dura Europus, in Syria, which was first excavated in the 1930s.[27] This church, known to be built in 236AD, delineates three distinct areas of community activity: the altar for the Eucharistic worship, the baptistry, and a third room believed to be a gathering room which would also have held the offerings brought by the faithful to be distributed by the Church to the poor of the community. Architectural study of the church of Ostica (Italy—4th c.), indicates that a large room existed for the collection of offerings of the faithful.[28]

During the Byzantine period, many church buildings had a large, specially designated room known as the *skeuphylakion*, which served as a repository for the material gifts offered by the faithful in addition to the storage of other items used in the performance of the sacred rites.[29] While not developed as thoroughly as other auxiliary buildings in the Orthodox worship space, such as the baptistry, the skeuphylakion was conceivably the first place that worshipers might visit when arriving to attend the liturgical services. Here they would bring their offerings, notably bread, wine, oil and money. A portion of these offerings would be selected for use in the sacred Liturgy, being transferred to the altar by the deacons in what would eventually become the Great Entrance ritual of the Divine Liturgy. After the deposition of the bread and wine on the holy table, the anaphoral eucharistic prayers would be offered by the bishop; then, the faithful would receive the sacred gifts (Holy Communion). The balance of the material gifts offered would be maintained for the sustenance of the clergy and for distribution to the poor.[30] The fourth canon of the Canons of the Holy Apostles (4th c.) instructs in this way: "Let all other fruits be sent home as first fruits for the bishops and presbyters, but not offered at the altar. But the bishops and presbyters should of course give a share of these things to the deacons, and the rest of the clergy."[31] This instruction echoes the teaching of the Church going back to the first century in the *Didache* concerning the sustenance of the spiritual leadership of the community.

Spiritual Economics in Medieval Christian Cultures— East and West

The rise of the Byzantine Empire[32] in the East radically transformed many aspects of Church life, including the nature of the Church as an offering community. The most obvious was the declaration by Constantine of the freedom of Christianity and the subsequent alliance of the Byzantine state with Orthodox Christianity.[33] Over the course of the Byzantine millennium, the uneasy alliance of church and state eventually resulted in state (tax) funding of certain aspects of Church life.[34] This development brought new financial resources to the Church, but threatened to compromise the central importance of Christian giving by all of the faithful. Schaff notes:

> [Constantine] not only restored (in 313) the buildings and estates, which had been confiscated in the Diocletian persecution, but granted the church also the right to receive legacies (321), and himself made liberal contributions in money and grain to the support of the clergy and the building of churches in Africa, in the Holy Land, in Nicomedia, Antioch, and Constantinople. Though this, be it remembered, can be no great merit in an absolute monarch, who is lord of the public treasury as he is of his private purse, and can afford to be generous at the expense of his subjects. He and his successors likewise gave to the church the heathen temples and their estates and the public property of heretics; but these more frequently were confiscated to the civil treasury or squandered on favorites. Wealthy subjects, some from pure piety, others from motives of interest, conveyed their property to the church, often to the prejudice of the just claims of their kindred.[35]

What evolved and emerged at this time was a rather robust system of patronage through which the Church (including monasteries) often exercised a key role in the way of life of medieval society. Patronage contributions by the wealthy and courtiers sometimes had something other than a spiritual meaning, being a means to a political end. This was not always the case, however, as gifts of generosity were often exemplary in the lives of Christians in positions of power, notably women.

Tithes Become Taxes in the Western Christian Empire

Eventually, under the edicts of Justinian, Theodosius and later emperors, certain financial relationships and interdependencies of Church and state were codified. In the West, a tithe for the support of the clergy was *mandated* at local councils at Tours (567) and Macon (585). By the middle of the eighth century, Charlemagne dictated that a tithe to be collected on behalf of the Church,

> Likewise, in accordance with the mandate of God, we command that all shall give a tithe of their property and labor to the churches and priests; let the nobles as well as the freemen…according to that which God shall have given to each Christian, return a part to God.[36]

In the West, this was only the beginning; William Tite comments on the development of the tithe in the West:

> Tithes were, by that enactment, to be applied to the maintenance of the bishop and clergy, the poor, and the fabric of the Church. In course of time the principle of payment of tithes was extended far beyond its original intention. Thus they became transferable to laymen and saleable like ordinary property, in spite of the injunctions of the third Lateran Council, and they became payable out of sources of income which were not originally tithable. The canon law contains numerous and minute provisions on the subject of tithes. The Decretum forbade their alienation to lay proprietors, denounced excommunication against those who refused to pay, and based the right of the Church upon scriptural precedents.[37]

In the East, the Byzantine pattern became normative for the Slavs as well, when they received Christianity in the 10th century. A similar pattern of state-Church interdependence developed and was normative until the rise of Communism in Eastern Europe in the 20th century.[38]

In a sense, much of the Church's financial well-being came to depend upon the effectiveness of the state's tax collection system.[39] The faithful were still strongly encouraged to continue the practice of free-will material offerings (or the exercise of charity). Schaff cites a certain discomfort among some of the great Fathers of the Church, seeing the wealth in their Churches, and quotes John Chrysostom,

> "The treasure of the church should be with you all, and it is only your hardness of heart that requires her to hold earthly property and to deal in houses and lands. Ye are unfruitful in good works, and so the ministers of God must meddle in a thousand matters foreign to their office.... Your fathers would have preferred that you should give alms of your incomes, but feared that your avarice might leave the poor to hunger; hence the present order of things."[40]

As the system of state support for Churches developed, charitable offerings by the faithful (particularly the wealthy) were no longer the sole means of financial support for ongoing life of the Church. At the same time, increasing financial resources were necessarily targeted to meet the practical needs of the Church—including building maintenance and support of the clergy.[41]

A tithe was normative in Armenian Churches as well, as attested by Krikor Maksoudian,

> Dues or taxes such as the tithe were also well known in the Byzantine Empire, in Armenia and in ancient Middle Eastern countries. In addition to the tithe, the Armenians also had other kinds of dues or taxes, as well as fines, the income from which was used for the maintenance of churches, monasteries, schools and the clergy.[42]

It would appear that a shift between Eastern and Western practice may have taken place at this point. In the East, the Church would be supported in part by the Empire through offerings and patronage, while in the West, the Church eventually became complicit in the collection of a tithe, which became, over time, like a tax exacted from the people, while the Church would provide certain services to the poor and the sick with the proceeds.[43]

Although the endowment of lands and grand gifts to the Church goes back to the apostolic age, with the rise of Byzantium, the Church became the recipient of extraordinary grand donations made by the Byzantine courtesans. These donations of entire churches,[44] monasteries and shrines to the Church became normative during the Byzantine Empire.[45]

In tenth-century Kievan Rus, St. Volodymyr made similar offerings, naming one of the churches built from his offering of a tenth of his wealth the 'Church of the All-Holy Tithe' (*Desyatynna Tserkva*).[46] In recognizing these dynamics of the first millennium, it is important to note the absence of a middle class in such cultures. In effect, if the churches had not been built by the wealthy, they would not have been built at all.

In psychological terms, these highly visible offerings of the wealthy may also have had a certain adverse effect; grand gifts may have effectively rendered the small and seemingly insignificant offerings of the poor 'meaningless'. The offering of extraordinary gifts, while present in the beginning in the Acts 5 account of the offering of the lands of Barnabas and Ananias and Sapphira, would manifest itself in Orthodox Church life throughout the ages. In the case of the Acts community, it was an encouragement, but not so in all cases. Less wealthy Christians might be tempted to assume that the practical needs of the Church were to be supported by someone else, either the state or the wealthy, as it had always been. Such a conclusion, based on pragmatic 'reality', fails to recognize the underlying spiritual nature of the righteous offering.

Church Stewardship as Management of Temporal Affairs

As mentioned above, when the Church received offerings from the faithful, they were applied to the needs of the Church, in charity to the poor and administration of the activities of the Church at large. Stewardship in this regard is not simply the *offering* of the gifts, but also in the wise *management* of these financial gifts, to be used in a manner consistent with the ethical teaching of the Church. This managerial role was deemed important in the Church, so much so that Canon XXVI of the Council of Chalcedon specified that every bishop should designate qualified individuals (from among the clergy) to manage the temporal affairs of the Church. This position, called the *oikonomos*, was to assure that the "goods of the church may not be squandered, nor reproach be brought upon the priesthood."[47]

Other positions of authority were present in Byzantine Church life to manage the affairs of the Church. For example, the management of lands was assigned to a *paramonarius* who may also have had a function in the management of certain functions in the church temple.[48] In Africa, a similar position came into existence, known as the *defensore,* who typically advocated for the legal rights of the poor, in addition to practical management of church property.[49] In Constantinople, the *skeuophylax* (sacristan) of Hagia Sophia had a position of extraordinary authority, having responsibility for the administration of the Patriarchal treasury. In an effort to exercise broad and effective stewardship, the Church created structures and clerical positions to manage these temporal affairs with a particular focus on the care of the poor. Except for the administration of funds offered to the monasteries, the bishop had oversight of all financial assets, including all church properties, but entrusted the details of management of these affairs to qualified clergy.[50]

Christian Offerings: The Path to Holiness and Monasticism

The first concern of Orthodox pastoral care is the salvation of souls. Avarice, covetousness and stinginess are sinful behaviors and attitudes that inhibit the work of divine grace in the human soul. A key component of the Orthodox Church's approach over history to the issue of stewardship was her pastoral concern for souls, warning about these spiritual evils and encouraging Christian generosity and love. Countless treatises and exhortations of the Fathers exist that speak to the inner dynamics of these sinful tendencies (passions) in the soul, and the spiritual remedies for healing. The influences of monasticism were strong in this regard as well, for most of the Fathers themselves were monks.[51] Given this orientation, the Orthodox Church would never be consumed with a pragmatic approach to increasing generosity in giving for practical purposes; rather, generosity was seen as a call to participation in the salvific grace of the Holy Spirit in one's soul. Stories abound of the saints who gave all they had to the poor (or to the Church on behalf of the poor) in order to live in humility and simple charity.[52]

The rise of monasticism had a profound effect upon Church governance in the Patristic age, not only because of the monasteries and monastic life itself, but by the fact that after the fourth century, all bishops were selected from the monastic communities. The tendency of the monastic movement was the orientation from the things of this world to spiritual things and the *eschaton*. This resulted in a type of 'spiritualization' of material things, where earthly things were viewed more in terms of a metaphorical representation of spiritual things. The monastic fathers, who had renounced the world, were often the ones preaching and teaching as bishops and monastic elders. Hence there tended to be less emphasis on the here and now, and more on what was present in the spiritual realm and the ultimate fulfillment in the heavenly realm.

One area in which the writings of the Fathers reflect this process is in the notion of the offering of firstfruits. One early witness to this spiritual theme is St. Methodius of Olympus in the third century, who likens the consecration of one's body and soul in virginity to be a sacred offering in fulfillment of the biblical mandate:

> "Virginity is something supernaturally great, wonderful, and glorious. To speak plainly and in accordance with the Holy

Scriptures, this best and noblest manner of life is alone the root of immortality—as well as its flower and first fruits. And for this reason, the Lord promises that those who have made themselves eunuchs shall enter into the Kingdom of Heaven... Celibacy among humans is a very rare thing and difficult to attain . . .For we must think of virginity as walking upon the earth—yet also reaching up to Heaven."[53]

Similarly, we hear St. Gregory Nazianzus preach:

Let us then carry our firstfruits to Him who has suffered and risen for us. Do you think perhaps that I am talking of gold, silver, garments or precious stones? Insubstantial earthly goods, transitory, tied to earth, owned for the most part by the wicked, the slaves of materialism and the prince of this world? No let us offer ourselves, it is the most precious and dearest gift in the eyes of God. Give to his image what resembles it most. Recognizing our greatness, honor our model, understanding the force of this mystery and the reasons for Christ death... Give all, offer all, to Him who has given Himself for us as a prize and ransom. We will give nothing as great as ourselves if we have grown by the nature of this mystery and have become for him all which he has become for us."[54]

One of the most influential Fathers of the Desert, St. Makarios speaks thusly,

The Patriarch Abraham, when he was receiving Melchisedek, the priest of God, made him an offering from the firstfruits of the earth and so obtained his blessing. Through this incident, the Spirit indicates that the first and highest elements of our constitution - the intellect, the conscience, the loving power of the soul - must initially be offered to God as a holy sacrifice. The first fruits and the highest of our true thoughts must be continually devoted to the remembrance of Him, engrossed in His love and in unutterable and boundless longing for him. In this way we can grow and move forward day by day, assisted by divine grace. Then the burden of fulfilling the commandments will appear light to us, and we will carry them out faultlessly and irreproachably, helped by the Lord Himself on account of our faith in Him.[55]

In these examples, the consecration of soul and intent is identified with the offering of the first fruits, in the latter case specifically as a fulfillment of the Genesis account of Melchizedek. In neither case is the offering of material things seen to be of specific value.[56]

Other Fathers, such as St. Cyprian of Carthage, spoke to the offering of alms as a sacrificial offering to the Lord:

> When we have pity on the poor, we are lending to God at interest, and when we give to the lowly, we are giving to God, in a spiritual sense, we are sacrificing a sweet fragrance to Him.[57]

This would become a common theme among the Fathers, as entire treatises by Chrysostom and others would use the offering/ firstfruits imagery to describe this offering, the poor being the recipients and the 'altar' of this offering to God.

The embodiment of stewardship as offering and charity in daily life in the lives of the saints became a model for all Christians. The Slavonic *Izbornik of 1076* is instructive in the view that offerings to God have a deep spiritual character and are the responsibility of faithful Christians.[58] The *Izbornik* is of particular importance because it reveals the Orthodox practice and belief at the emergence of corporate Slavonic Orthodox spiritual life - with its roots in Byzantine Christianity, the patristic sources and the scriptures themselves.[59] For example, the *Izbornik* restates the Wisdom of Sirach extensively in its references to the nature of spiritual offerings:

> If one offers sacrifice from unrighteousness, the offering is blemished, nor will sin be forgiven for a multitude of sacrifices. Like he who kills a son in front of his father is he who offers a sacrifice from the property of the poor... Do not appear before the Lord empty handed, for all this is for the commandment's sake. The offering of the righteous

anoints the altar, and its fragrance rises before the Most High… Glorify God with what is good, and do not stint the first fruits of your hands, and dedicate your tithe with gladness. Give to the Most High as He has given, for the Lord is the one who repays and He will repay you sevenfold. He who loves gold will not be justified, and he who loves what is corruptible will be filled himself. Many have come to ruin because of gold and their destruction was before their face.[60]

Here the spiritual guidance of Sirach is selectively applied as spiritual guidance for Christians, specifically as it regards the offering of sacrifices and care of the poor. Similarly, in the section titled, 'A Certain Father's Words to His Son for Profit of His Soul', a wonderful passage on charity gives a theology of Orthodox *praxis* at the time,

Do not say of your possessions, "They are mine," but say, "They are entrusted to me for a few days," and like a steward disburse what is entrusted to you as He who gave it in trust to you will order. Thus what the Most High has given to you, make it the possession of the Most High in Him. Do not leave it for your descendants, but give your children and your wife and your entire family up to God, the good Keeper whose mercy is great and whose wealth is unfathomable. For the possessions of this world are like a river: it runs down here and comes back again from above. Now if inhabitants upstream, instead of choosing not to fill their cups to the brim and refraining from sating fully their cattle, saying, "Let us leave it for the inhabitants downstream, and let us take only a little," draw, on the contrary, water in excess and care not for those downstream, the river will fail them as well. Thus do not have concern for the possessions of your descendents, of your sons, grandsons, great-grandsons, or daughters, for the time will treat them diversely with catastrophes, or robbery, or war, and then what is lost will be of no avail to them. Therefore, in your lifetime, think of your soul and care for it earnestly, for you have only one soul, one lifetime, and one death…

> If you were to use the riches of this world to pay for one of
> the least dwellings of the Jerusalem on high, not even the
> entire riches of this world taken together would pay for its
> value. It is with charity that the kingdom of God is bought,
> charity which lies not in great or frequent or small giving, but
> in the means of the giver and his whole heart.[61]

The spiritual sense of this passage recalls the teachings of Christ regarding the laying up of treasures in heaven (Mt. 6:19-21). Here the wise father teaches the Orthodox perspective of the whole of life as stewardship, and the spiritual 'offering of the family' is central to this understanding.[62] Similarly, material possessions, owned by God, can become offerings of charity to the poor and lead to spiritual treasure that is eternal.

As in every area of sinful human life, the *praxis* of individual Christians and the institutional Church is invariably uneven, often 'missing the mark' of the ideals of Orthodox spirituality and practice.[63] The canonical tradition reflects certain practical efforts to direct the life of the Church regarding the detrimental effects of the mismanagement of money in the Church. The very existence of canons that speak to the matters of simony, dissemination of episcopal estates and similar matters indicates that these spiritual ideals were often not lived in practice.[64] Over its first seventeen centuries, the life of the Orthodox Church as a whole was directed by these principles of stewardship, even if these ideals of Christian stewardship were not fully implemented in practice.

Closely related to the Christian call to offering is the Christian vocation to take responsibility (stewardship) for one's neighbor— particularly those in need. Hence, the Church, from the beginning, prompted her faithful to give generously to those in need and to set up ministry structures to care for those needs.[65] Very early, the Church recognized its responsibility to care for widows and orphans, and eventually established a special order for young, unmarried women. Prior to Constantine, the resources used for these ministries were funded directly from the donations of the faithful. As noted above, Justin Martyr's account of the collection of the early Church at the liturgy earmarks the goods for those in need.

During the Byzantine period, the Church took on an active role of dispensing the charity for the welfare and betterment of those in need. Many of the great Fathers of the Church, (e.g. St. John Chrysostom, St. Basil the Great) were bishops who became renowned for their establishment of charitable service ministries for the poor and the sick, including hospitals and houses (*ptochokemia*) for the poor and travelers.[66] Even in the post-Byzantine era, the Church continued to serve actively in this role under the Ottomans.[67] The Church was the advocate of the poor—which included most of the disenfranchised Christians living under Islamic rule.

There existed a sense, in the Byzantine Empire, that the Emperor and those endowed with wealth were responsible for Godly stewardship of their wealth, in charity to the poor. Exemplary in this effort was the life of John II Batatzes (1222-54) (son of Emperor Theodore Laskaris) who is called 'the Almsgiver'.[68] John's charity was known far and wide throughout the empire. Ruth Macrides describes this charitable work:

> *Eleemosyne* is one of the virtues which every *philanthropos basileus* was expected to possess…The emperor founded churches, hospitals, orphanages, old-age homes, and still left reserves in the treasure and piles of provisions heaped high in towers. Money for these foundations was not squeezed from the people but amassed by the emperor's careful management. Pachymeres tells us that on one occasion when the emperor was ill and could not obtain help from doctors; in imitation of God's *eleos* he gave sacks of gold coins to the needy. The emperor asked the patriarch to testify to the fact that the money was not from the public treasury but from the emperor's own savings.[69]

In Byzantium, the synergy of Church and state was meant to work in harmony in bringing God's blessing to the people of God's house (*oikos*), especially the poor. The right oversight of that house (*oikonomia*) required cooperation between church and state that was seriously lacking at times.

While a thorough discussion of stewardship in the Kievan Church in the second millennium cannot be addressed here, several points do need to be made.[70] At first, in Rus, the Church-state modeled itself on the Byzantine structure, but the dominance of the Church by imperial powers seriously changed the dynamics of offering in churches.[71] Direct state support (and to a degree, control) of the Church would become normative as it was in much of western Europe, but funding of church construction, maintenance and clerical support would not necessarily be a priority, particularly in times of civil strife or invasion.

Secondly, on the western frontier of Kievan Rus (Ukraine) and those areas that subsequently came under Polish (or Austro-Hungarian) control, the material situation of the Orthodox people and their churches became dire.[72] The Church infrastructure was decimated by the move of the Metropolitanate of Kiev to Vladimir as the territory was overrun by the invasion of the Tartars. Further erosion resulted from the ecclesiastical mismanagement of certain bishops and clergy who used their offices more for personal gain than pastoral service.

In the 1588-89 Patriarch Joachim II of Antioch personally toured these Ukrainian lands and encouraged a renewal of the church locally by the lay brotherhoods, which provided leadership and financial support for the local Orthodox Church in the face of local mismanagement by the clergy.[73] Given a mandate to effect change in the life of the Kievan Church by the Patriarchate of Constantinople, the brotherhoods became powerful ecclesiastical forces for Orthodoxy.[74] Some brotherhoods were chartered in such a way so as to report directly to the Patriarch of Constantinople and not to local bishops.[75] In this scenario, the incompetence of local bishops resulted in the abrogation of their role as ecclesiastical stewards of important elements of Church life to (often) dedicated and competent laymen. This turn of events would establish the lay brotherhoods as a formidable force in Ukrainian Church life for centuries. They provided much of the benefice to the Church locally, including financing church affairs, charitable works and printing liturgical books. The rise of the lay brotherhoods would set a pattern for later clergy—lay dynamics that sometimes became characteristic of Ukrainian Orthodox parish life when the Church was planted in America three centuries later.

Even in imperial Russia, save for the clergy at the highest levels, the financial status of the priests serving parishes was impoverished, if not desperate. Bishop Tikhon (Fitzgerald),[76] of the OCA Diocese of San Francisco and the West, quotes Gregory Freeze in describing their life and the necessity of establishing the system of fees to compensate clergy through offerings provided when they performed ministrations:

> "By the time of [Czar] Nicholas' accession in 1825, the parish clergy still depended entirely upon their traditional sources of support: emoluments, holiday collections, and cultivation of parish-church land. A few churches enjoyed some other forms of support: cathedrals had small subsidies from the state, and some urban churches and small capital endowments or rent from real estate bequeathed by parishioners. In very rare instances the clergy too enjoyed fixed support--mainly in kind and known as RUGA--usually provided in lieu of land or because of the parish's small size. In most parishes, however, the clergy enjoyed no such support and had to depend on the traditional emoluments and parish land for sustenance. That support, as both Church and state authorities agreed, showed major weaknesses…"

> "To begin with, the monetary income from emoluments was simply inadequate. The clergy themselves, in their annual written reports, often described the income from gratuities as 'scanty,' occasionally as 'average,' very rarely as 'satisfactory.' The clergy's superiors, like the bishop of Penza, confirmed such negative assessments: 'The parish clergy receive no more than one hundred rubles in the very best parishes (here) as monetary income, and on the average they receive no more than fifty rubles, or even thirty rubles, per annum.'"[77]

Bishop Tikhon goes on to state that, "clergy of those distant times and now most foreign places tended (or rather were forced) by appalling circumstances) to set minimum rates for their accomplishment of such routine, ordinary, essential, typical, customary, habitual, usual services as crownings, burials, baptisms, house-blessings, Panachidas, moliebens, etc., etc."[78] The bishop's intent in the letter was to emphasize that while such practices emerged out of desperation and became common in the past and in foreign lands, they are not to be considered normative in the least in his diocese in America.[79] Nevertheless, the new Slavic immigrants to America would see this system payment for services rendered as normal and establish it in the new order of church life in the New World as well.

The historical practices of Orthodox stewardship as manifest in liturgical offering, construction of church facilities, charity to the poor, Church financial management, the spiritual tradition on charity, etc. had a rich and diverse history in the first seventeen centuries of Orthodox Christianity. Yet the implementation of these principles and practices would encounter new challenges when immersed in the American milieu.

CHAPTER FIVE

THE EFFECTS OF WESTERN PRACTICES ON ORTHODOX STEWARDSHIP IN THE AMERICAN CHRISTIAN MILIEU

Stewardship Practices in Non-Orthodox American Congregations

In the West[1], the winds of the Reformation would signal a storm of change in ecclesial life in Europe during the 15th – 18th centuries and the emergence of new philosophical ideas in society, notably Rationalism and Capitalism. This storm would blow the seeds of new religious communities (uprooted from European strife) westward, and plant new Christian communities in the religious soil of the New World where they could grow, fed by the freedom of religious expression and liberation from persecution encountered in Europe.

Before addressing the situation in the United States, however it might be helpful to note the state of affairs in England in the early 16th century, which would quickly set the pattern for the management of Church-state affairs in the Colonies. Notably, the dissolution of the Catholic Church in England and the rise of Henry VIII was accompanied by a radical reorientation of Church life as Catholic monastic institutions and Churches were dissolved by edict and the wealth of the monasteries confiscated. Because the monasteries were an important foundation stone of medieval life, this change caused radical, unforeseen changes, notably an extensive rise in societal poverty, because the monks and nuns had routinely used their land and material resources to care for the large numbers of the sick and poor.[2] This disruption of the synergy of monasticism and its care for the poor, present since the fourth century in part, ripped the fabric of civilization in this emerging period as a result of the Reformation mindset. The unsettled political circumstances of Western Europe in the sixteenth and seventeenth centuries led, in part, to the establishment of the Colonies themselves, as certain communities devoid of political power could only find religious freedom or even an existence in the New World.

Eventually, the landscape of American religious life in the eighteenth and nineteenth centuries would be marked by a multitude of groups *competing* for preeminence, in what Roger Finke and Rodney Stark refer to as a 'religious economy.'[3] Fink and Stark describe the dynamics of religious economy:

> We see religious affiliation as a matter of choice, religious organizations must compete for members and that the "invisible hand" of the marketplace is as unforgiving for ineffective religious firms as it is for their commercial counterparts…

> Religious economies are like commercial economies in that they consist of a market made up of a set of current and potential customers and a set of firms seeking to serve that market. The fate of these firms will depend upon (1) aspects of their organizational structures, (2) their sales representatives, (3) their product, and (4) their marketing techniques. Translated into more churchly language, the relative success of religious bodies (especially when confronted with an unregulated economy) will depend upon their polity, their clergy, their religious doctrines, and their evangelization techniques.[4]

They describe a sect-to-church process of growth, whereby, "successful religious movements nearly always shift their emphasis toward this world and away from the next."[5] It is into this ever-changing religious landscape that the Orthodox Church would eventually find herself immersed.

Generally speaking, in Colonial America, the original founding groups grew in wealth and influence in their prospective lands. With this growth came a rise of secularization, as affluence grew and the zeal for the spiritual principles of the Church waned. Finke and Stark put it this way:

> In time, however, successful sects come to be dominated by the more successful—those for whom life's pleasures are options. And thus begins the gradual accommodation to the world…Successful religious movements nearly always shift their emphasis toward this world and away from the next, moving from high tension with the environment to lower levels of tension. As this occurs, a religious body will become increasingly less able to satisfy members who desire a higher tension version of faith. As discontent grows, these people will begin to complain that the group is abandoning its original positions and practices, as indeed it has. At some point this growing conflict with the group will erupt in a split and the faction desiring a return to higher tension will leave to found a new sect.[6]

This process has important ramifications for personal and ecclesial stewardship; it is based on a shift in the emphasis toward this world and away from the next. If such a shift does occur, fundamental elements of personal spiritual commitment as reflective of a life of Christian stewardship may be supplanted by other, more worldly principles. Some of these dynamics among Orthodox groups will be examined later in this discussion.

Establishment and Disestablishment of 'State Churches' in the West

In one sense, the European model would continue to prevail for some time in America; some of the states had 'established' Churches, which worked cooperatively with state governments in a mutually, financially supportive relationship.[7] Writings from the period indicate an extensive (and often despised) system for collecting 'tithes' from everyone, including church members.[8]   To capture a sense of the time, Frederick Mark Gedicks notes the following:

> Many of the repressive attributes of the Anglican establishment in England were replicated in the colonies. Under the Anglican establishment in Virginia, for example—the "most rigid and exclusive establishment of religion in America"—the Church of England enjoyed the benefit of land grants, financial support by a mandatory tithe, enforcement of compulsory Anglican worship, and the harassment and prohibition of religious competitors. Baptist, Congregationalist, and Roman Catholic clergy were routinely fined and imprisoned, and were subject to summary expulsion from the colony. Quakers were frequently subjected to imprisonment and expulsion, and Roman Catholics were prohibited from holding public office. Between 1720 and 1750, more Virginians were indicted for failing to attend Anglican services than for any other crime, with evasion of mandatory tithes a close second.[9]

In Connecticut, the Congregationalists enjoyed similar established status and privileges from the relationship.

The disestablishment of the established churches in the nineteenth century in America may have been the good news; the new challenges to maintain church structures required new approaches to financial management, and new efforts to rediscover the meaning of stewardship in the Christian life.[10]   However, not all was progress. One sign of the process of secularization and decline was the rise of a certain lamentable materialism, as reported by Frederick A. Norwood regarding the Methodists in the mid-nineteenth century:

> ...[I]n their desire to raise money for the benefit of the church, they have recourse to selling pews to the highest bidder; to parties of pleasure, oyster suppers, fairs, grab-bags, festivals and lotteries... The New School Methodists appear to depend upon the patronage of the worldly, the favor of

the proud and aspiring; and the various artifices of worldly policy.[11]

John Wesley had foreseen these developments, trying to construct a solution for the tension between material wealth and spiritual decline.

> Religion must necessarily produce both industry and frugality, and these cannot but produce riches. So as riches increase, so will pride, anger and love of the world in all its branches... We ought not to prevent people from being diligent and frugal; we must exhort all Christians to gain all they can, and save all they can—this is, in effect, to grow rich. What way, then can we take, that our money may not sink us into the nethermost hell? There is one way, and there is no other way under heaven. If those who gain all they can, save all they can, will likewise give all they can, then the more they will grow in grace, and the more treasure they lay up in heaven.[12]

In multi-denominational America a tension developed between established Churches and a variety of newly emerging upstart 'sects', such as the Methodists and Baptists. Eventually the original established churches in most areas began to lose considerable ground to these upstart groups that had the capability of growing quickly and fluidly. Finke and Stark track the reasons for success in the struggle of the upstart denominations; they grow until their own structures evolve to the point where they lose their competitive edge in the religious marketplace, resulting in secularization and decline.[13]

Funding the work of the Church (including missionary expansion) was one area in which the religious economy was quite effective in sorting out religious priorities of congregations in new territories. The upstart denominational groups had a distinct advantage in requiring less initial funding. One major expense to established churches was a requirement for seminary-educated clergy, and a subsequent stipend suitable to the clergyman's considerable education.[14] The upstart sects tended to have a sacrificial character.[15] Stewardship itself became a topic for prompting evangelization among certain revivalistic sects of the mid-19th century. In this view, Christian stewardship was seen as the "consecration of the money power of the church to God."[16] There developed no consensus among American Protestants as to whether or not a minimum tithe (ten percent offering) was to be required of the faithful, the confusion perhaps due to the confusion of the mandatory 'tithe' in established churches with a voluntary spiritual tithe. Among those who believed that the faithful should tithe were those who considered the Old Testament mandates to be directly applicable to the Christian era.[17] For these believers, a ten percent offering should be normative, because tithing was prescribed by God in the Bible. Others interpreted the new dispensation in Christ to effectively abrogate the 'old law' of which tithing was a part, and to continue to follow it was viewed, by these interpreters, as a denial of the saving work of Christ and even an attempt to please God through 'works.' Some Protestant commentators saw the development of the prescribed tithe as part of the decline of the Church after the initial period of ecclesial purity characteristic of the apostolic era, which was subsequently corrupted during the Byzantine era.[18] For them, the offering response was to be disconnected from any sense of duty or obligation and based instead on personal choice and generosity of soul alone.

The Influences of Capitalism and Pragmatism

One's view of wealth has a considerable impact on one's view of stewardship of that wealth. The influence of capitalism as the operative principle in American economic philosophy had a profound influence on Protestant America's vision of life and stewardship in the eighteenth and nineteenth centuries, and in our own age as well. A tension developed between those theologies which hail frugality and simplicity as virtues and the emergent capitalistic model, which promotes wealth generation as a good and worthy end for human endeavors (and essentially God-given).[19]

While the effects of an emerging capitalism on the American view of wealth is of interest, equally pertinent to the subject is the sense of the capitalistic *way of thinking* in regard to the free choice of religion itself. Finke and Stark describe participation in religious groups in capitalistic terms of costs, benefits, risks and rewards in the religious marketplace. In religious communities, they note the human tendency of leaders to decrease the cost of entry into membership and maintaining membership.[20] This tendency can result in disillusion for those who have already 'paid a price' and results in discontent or defection.[21] However, one observable phenomenon happens relative to stewardship in such cases—those who have paid the price may stop paying the tithe / offering as well if there are shifts in the behaviors of the church system. It has not been uncommon in a democratic setting to have to deal with large groups of people who refuse to contribute their assessment to the denominational leadership body.[22] In doing so they are exercising their capitalistic management (stewardship?) in those areas that they have rationally deemed worthy of their personal concern and investment. In capitalistic religious spheres of influence, money can again become the currency of power and influence.

A related philosophy of American life that affects stewardship is a type of pragmatism that places a premium on measurable results and tangible works. In churches, congregational decision-making might be influenced by such a philosophy when it comes to fiscal management, church growth, clergy compensation, ministry funding etc. A pragmatic approach might favor 'brick and mortar' projects that produce visible results, as opposed to certain spiritual endeavors that might have a far less measurable effect. Likewise, there can be an emphasis on numbers of souls or church congregations or amounts of money donated, with less regard to the inner intangible character (faith commitment, spiritual growth, etc.) of those who are so counted. In the end, even mission work must be paid for and the decisions to embark on spiritual missionary activities may depend on the availability of even nominal financial resources. Pragmatism will often decide which priorities get funded.[23]

Contemporary American Protestant Trends and Practices

Since the mid-nineteenth century, stewardship as a subject unto itself has been a topic of great interest in Protestant Churches in America. Numerous programs of stewardship awareness, tithing, Bible study, fund-raising and financial management exist across the spectrum. Some recent contemporary approaches to stewardship have tended to emphasize advocacy for the poor and environmentalism— even decrying capitalistic systems as fundamentally unjust and enslaving to the poor. In this view, capitalism is seen to fuel the flames of excess acquisition and rampant materialism.

However, there are dissenting voices to this frame of thinking in the discussion. One interesting take on the issue comes from John R. Schneider, who presents biblical arguments that Christians should enjoy wealth as a sign of the favor of God.[24] By basing his analysis on certain Lukan biblical themes, Schneider contends that, "just as there is a spirituality for being poor, there is a spirituality for being rich."[25] He contends that, for some, "it is affluence that …leads people to God."[26] In this view, the wealth bestowed upon Christians can be seen as a blessing by God; "Jesus envisioned his mission as a cosmic jubilee and ultimate day of release for the poor."[27] These God-given resources are meant to raise the impoverished (socially). While Schneider is very measured in his analysis of the economic systems of the early Church, a more simplistic approach is the 'Prosperity Gospel' which arose in a simplified form in the late 19th century and advocated by some contemporary preachers who equate wealth with the bestowal of God's favor and encourage their followers to 'claim' their inheritance from God in a monetary way.[28]

Despite the intensive efforts of American Protestant churches to develop theologies and systems of implementing stewardship principles in their congregations, the financial resources of many such church bodies are in decline. Major declines in income (paralleling or matching declines in membership) have led to cuts in staffing and missionary projects in many mainline denominations.[29] Writing in the 1980s, Douglas Hall notes that contemporary interest in the notion of stewardship is primarily an American phenomenon; it is practically unknown in Europe. Unlike many of the European parent denominational authorities, church bodies in North America (save for the early established churches) have had to fend for themselves, without governmental support.[30]

Roman Catholic Developments in America

While Protestantism was the predominant force of American religious life from the beginning of European colonization, Roman Catholicism had its own trajectory of growth and development in America, affected in part by similar dynamics as its Protestant predecessors. Finke and Stark describe American Catholicism in its formation as 'an Irish sect movement' with characteristic strengths of strong sacrificial elements and identification with the Church.[31] They credit the "intense faith with a vivid sense of otherworldliness" for much of the success in maintaining their identity in the religiously diverse and sometimes antagonistic American religious scene in which they were immersed.[32]

The Catholic churches developed a different system of financial stewardship than the Protestant churches. A critical step in this development was the defeat of an emergent congregational parish structure in Roman Catholicism in Maryland by the Second Plenary Council of Baltimore in 1866.[33] As a result, the Catholic hierarchy, (primarily ethnically Irish) succeeded in establishing a uniformity of Church life throughout the United States and a system of diocesan central control of funds quite unlike decentralized Protestant systems.

Because of the shared tradition of the first millennium of Christianity, stewardship principles in Roman Catholicism and Orthodoxy are similar. Sacrificial offerings made to the emerging Catholic Churches were critical to its initial success and ongoing growth. As the Catholic Churches in the nineteenth century consisting primarily of minority immigrants, the local parishes played multiple roles in maintaining community identity. However, as the needs of growing Catholic communities became more acute in the 20th century, the Catholic congregations routinely resorted to fund-raising practices similar to those lamented by the Methodists above, notably bingo and games of chance. These became common, if not normative, in many Catholic parishes by the late 1950s, particularly those supporting Catholic schools.

With the advent of Vatican Council II,[34] the Catholic Church in America has experienced extraordinary upheaval, resulting in fundamental changes in the dynamics of Church life, including the liturgy.[35] The establishment of lay parish leadership boards and attempts to engage the laity actively in ministries of the Church has created a new dynamic in financial stewardship in American Catholicism. In recent decades, stewardship programs have been developed which parallel similar Protestant programs, yet retaining a Roman Catholic quality.[36] In 1993, the American Catholic bishops addressed the issue of stewardship in a pastoral letter, delineating the spiritual underpinnings of stewardship as it relates to one's life in Christ.[37]   It is difficult to assess if, or the degree to which, such pronouncements and programs have made an impact on the American Catholic *praxis* of financial giving and management.

It is into this milieu that eastern Orthodoxy was planted, and has grown to its present state. This immersion into a western capitalistic, pragmatic, multi-ethnic, multi-denominational cultural ethos would bring new challenges to the fledgling Orthodox churches of the early 20th century. The freedom promoted in American culture to allow individuals to ratify a free choice of personal religious views and practices, from among a multitude of coexistent competing religious groups, would create the dynamic of an American religious economy—a situation quite different from the native lands of the early Orthodox immigrants.

Orthodoxy Arrives in America—*Oikonomia* in a Religious Economy

Orthodox Christianity arrived in America in two distinct movements - the initial arrival of Russian missionaries in Alaska in the late 18th century and their subsequent migration to Northern California, followed a century later by the great immigration from Eastern Europe, Greece and the Middle East in the late 19th and early 20th centuries. The initial Russian foray into Alaska was conducted by the Russian Empire, with funding support for local Russian Orthodox Church communities in the territories established to serve the Russian fur traders. While the initial interest of the Russian empire in Alaska was purely mercenary, the spiritual mission work was highly successful through the sacrificial efforts of saintly men who endeavored to bring the Gospel to the native Alaskans in their own language using their own motifs.[38] With the establishment of the Metropolia in San Francisco, the Russian mission continued to grow slowly, confronting the challenge posed by the sale of Alaska to the United States. By the time of the Russian Revolution, funds from the mother Church in Russia for the American mission dried up, resulting in a financial crisis for the fledgling Russian Orthodox presence in America.[39]

In terms of sheer numbers, the second movement, namely the arrival of immigrants from Eastern Europe and Orthodox Mediterranean nations, served to be a far more prolific source of new Orthodox Christians in America at the beginning of the 20th century.[40] It should be noted that there were distinct differences between the migrations of the Orthodox in the 19th-20th centuries and those of Protestant reformers 250 years earlier. The primary motivation for the migration of the Orthodox was to seek not religious freedom, but the improvement of personal financial well-being.[41] Like others of the period, these Orthodox immigrants, living in utter poverty in Europe, journeyed to America with great hope that their economic conditions and ability to support their families would improve.

Religiously, most of the Slavs who could be found in Orthodox Churches in the early 20th century arrived on these shores as Eastern Rite Catholics.[42] With the return of large numbers of Eastern Rite Catholics to Orthodoxy, first under the leadership of St. Alexis Toth, and through several similar subsequent movements, the Orthodox Church established its base for subsequent growth.[43] An examination of Orthodox Church structures from the period can be helpful in understanding the Church's current understanding and practice of stewardship.

Congregationalist Models of Leadership in Orthodox Churches

The creation of Congregationalist church structures in American Orthodoxy is a phenomenon that has profound implications on the exercise of stewardship in the contemporary Church. Fr. Nicholas Ferencz has investigated the formation of historical ecclesiastical structures in American Orthodoxy, notably the congregational model of church structure, and its impact on contemporary Orthodox ecclesiology.[44] Parallel to the formation of parish communities (and eventually jurisdictional Orthodox central authorities) are the practices (and attitudes) of giving and financial management that exemplified an emergent Congregationalist Orthodoxy in America. Of particular interest is the leadership role of the laity, who from the ground up gathered congregations, founded churches, collected donations and assisted their poor brethren among the newly arrived immigrants.[45] In many cases, these leaders were those who were successful locally as merchants, or leaders in other capacities (e.g. pit bosses or labor leaders.)[46] In the early years, because of a scarcity of ordained clergy and episcopal authorities to assign clergy, lay congregational leaders invited the priests to come to serve their communities from the Old Country, placing them in the position to set the priest's compensation and dismiss the priest as well. For some of the Orthodox who left the Eastern Rite Catholic churches, the move to Orthodoxy was an opportunity to reassert lay control over what was an increasingly controlled ecclesiastical environment dominated by diocesan bishops and centralized church structures. This attitude sometimes reflected a distrust of clergy or a certain atmosphere of anti-clericalism.[47]

Financial Management of Emerging American Orthodox Churches

John Erickson describes the historical evolution of a stewardship ethic in Orthodox churches during this early founding period.[48] The parishes were often formed by brotherhoods of men who gathered together to pool resources, raise funds, and begin a process of land acquisition to build churches.[49] This process was highly sacrificial. Erickson notes,

> Parishes...were not built by the tsar or even by large contributions from a handful of wealthy patrons. They were built by ordinary men and women who contributed generously from their own often meager resources. But even these ordinary men and women had to be asked to contribute.[50]

Clearly, a dynamic of sacrificial giving was at work in these Orthodox communities early in the twentieth century. However, the importance of this shift to lay financial leadership should not be underestimated. In these congregations, the finances of the parish were managed by elected church boards whose financial management systems were often borrowed from secular sources, rather than based in ecclesiastical stewardship principles. Constitutions were developed in parishes that delineated the roles of laity and, in many cases, limited the roles of priests and even bishops, in the management of temporal affairs. A clergy-laity polarization could quickly develop— reinforced by the parish constitution - that relegated the material affairs of the church to the lay boards and the spiritual affairs to the clergy.[51] This type of structure, normative in most Orthodox parishes of the early 20th century across the ethnic jurisdictions, mirrored extent structures of church life for existing Protestant churches.[52] In addition, the dynamics of church life in America (capitalism, pragmatism, congregationalism) as a religious economy, were formative in what would become Orthodox parish life as well.

Particularly among the Slavs, these early Orthodox and Eastern Rite Catholic communities faced serious challenges in the New

World—language, ethnic biases, poverty, misunderstandings, etc. One serious problem came from within—the strife of dealing with the internal community polarities of clergy-laity, Russian-Ukrainian, Catholic-Orthodox, even Galician chant style verses *Prostopenije.*[53] The democracy of the parish board system allowed these disagreements to percolate publicly and sometimes to become full blown arguments, particularly at parish Annual Meetings of the membership. The civil court system would often be called upon to resolve the resultant lawsuits and, in the end, congregations divided.[54] In these instances, community trust was destroyed, and where trust is absent, faithful stewardship, sharing and generosity is most likely obliterated.

Many Old World Orthodox and Eastern Rite Catholic immigrants who became Orthodox were seeking the American dream and were glad to have a stake in the possibility of exercising a new kind of personal responsibility and stewardship for their lives. In part, their New World experience was rooted in the empowerment that came from employment and earning money—shaking the bonds of abject poverty (or serfdom) in Eastern Europe, or impoverished life under the Ottomans. They now had a voice and they would use it.

From Free Will Offerings to the Parish Dues System

A new mechanism[55] of financial giving came into existence in many congregations with the establishment of systems of parish dues among many Orthodox parishes during the early 20th century.[56] The dues system was based on the pragmatic need to raise money to run the parish, build and maintain facilities and meet operational expenses while attempting to do so in a fair and equitable manner for all of the parishioners. Typically, at the annual meeting the parish board would set a fixed amount per capita (or family) that each parishioner would have to contribute to maintain his or her status as an active parish member. The dues system was often embedded in the written constitution of the parish and in some sense, legally binding upon the parish leadership to observe. The sum of the dues collected was calculated to meet the projected needs of parish operations for the year. In short, active membership in the Church came to be equated with financial payment.

It was not uncommon for leaders of the parish to go door-to-door to collect dues.[57] In situations where a family's financial need was acute, the payment of dues was not always strictly required for participation in Church liturgical life, but inevitably it would be required for participation in the annual meeting of members and (almost always) 'back dues' would have to be paid to the Church for someone who had not kept up annual payments, then died, in order for him or her to be buried from the Church.[58] The dues amount was a sign of the equality of parishioners and everybody paid the same amount. However, the system was not responsive to the real-life situation of those Orthodox Christians who were poor and for whom the dues payment was a substantial, if not unbearable, amount.[59]

Over time, it became increasingly difficult for parish leaders to raise minimum annual dues amounts despite the fact that inflationary expenses began to outrace parish dues income.[60] To meet shortfalls, parishes often reverted to other means of fund raising to garner the funds required to meet basic expenses. Parishes would form committees to set up food sales, hold parish festivals, or offer public games of chance to raise funds.[61] Often, the income of the parish from such fund raising schemes would far exceed the income from parish dues or free will offerings. In such cases, the surrounding community became the source of basic parish funding and the notion of personal responsibility/sacrificial offering was limited to the dues obligation and possibly an offering of time in the fund raising effort. The offering of one's time and effort in working fund raisers was viewed by some as preferable to making personal financial donations, but may well have a sacrificial element to it.[62]

Another effect of the dues system was the psychological effect that it had on parish donation practices. Dues, like taxes, were often viewed as inevitable, but distasteful. As people would rarely consider giving over and above their required taxes, so a similar pattern of thought emerges regarding the church dues. A legalistic minimalism toward church giving began to erode the original sacrificial generosity of the founding generation of the parish. Ironically, many parishioners could feel free to channel their charitable giving to worthy causes at work, social clubs, and fraternal organizations, but may have felt reluctant to contribute to the parish. While offerings for devotional candles served as a significant source of parish income; there was still a pragmatic aspect to this—the reception of something tangible for the offering.[63]

Another effect of the dues system has been the tendency to obscure the Christian spiritual focus on outreach to others, resulting in a myopic emphasis on the immediate circle of parish and core ethnic group, at the expense of the greater Christian vision of care and love for all. In some cases, parish auxiliary groups and brotherhoods (and sisterhoods) became the vehicles for expanding the circle beyond the immediate parish.[64]

In addition to serving as a type of financial stewardship, the dues system also was employed by some nationwide Orthodox jurisdictional bodies, who established systems of diocesan dues which continue to this day as a primary means of raising funds for the work of the diocese and staffing the consistory or diocesan offices.[65] The diocesan dues system became embedded in diocesan constitutions and normative in practice. However, the long-term effects on a diocesan level were similar to that in the parishes—enthusiasm for the supporting the diocesan structures waned. Jurisdictional Church councils experienced reluctance among its member-representatives to raise dues on the parishes, preferring instead that the jurisdictional leadership (laity and bishops) tighten the belt and do without.[66]

Similarly, the system of payment for services rendered known in the Old Country became common. While the priest often received his fee for services, the parish board sometimes exacted additional payments for use of the facilities, even the church building. While supposedly voluntary, these fees were exacted whenever one wished to approach the sacraments—baptisms, weddings, and even penance. In addition, to receive these benefits as a member in good standing, one's annual dues had to be paid as well, and in some cases, back dues from prior years. It is difficult to estimate (or underestimate) the harm done by such a system. At its worst, it is a form of established simony. Some people began to identify the payment with the sacrament.[67] In this system a significant portion of a priest's financial compensation and the well-being of his family might well be dependent upon such fees.

Has the dues-fees system been effective, even in a practical sense? Evidence from Church sources indicates that it worked only nominally at best. For example, Fr. Ferencz notes that the Mayfield, Pennsylvania *Sobor* of the Russian Orthodox Greek Catholic Church in 1907, headed by Metropolitan Tikhon, attempted to begin a reversal of the Congregationalist model of leadership in the parishes. Central to this process was a financial consideration: "plans to increase the parishioner contributions to the parish and pastors' salaries, and increase parish contributions to the diocese, were put off for future deliberation by a committee."[68] This episode indicates how difficult it was to raise minimum dues levels and resultant funds for the purpose of funding the broader goals of the Church jurisdictional structure. It would be a sign of future difficulties raising money as well. Regarding the Russian Orthodox Metropolia, Fr. Ferencz notes the inability of diocesan authorities to elicit sufficient financial support from the people "set the stage for the financial collapse of the diocese" in 1922.[69] Scott cites more recent statistics:

> Based on a recent national study, average annual giving as defined by 'dues' or a "pledge" by Greek Orthodox Christians to their church in North America averages approximately $300 per year. And this from the Orthodox cultural group most often identified with material success! This is among the lowest per capita giving among all American faith traditions. Many parishes persist in leveraging dues though it is described as "stewardship." This is the nominalism that haunts sacramental realism.[70]

From Free Will Offerings to Fund Raising

The dues system was not the sole means of acquiring income to meet parish needs. In some cases, special fund drives became common for large projects or extraordinary needs. In many cases, these drives were driven by pragmatic concerns—leaky roofs, financial shortfalls, hall renovations, etc. Often, donations were published and linked to specific (concrete) items. Many Slavic churches from the early twentieth century have stained glass windows that testify to the generosity of their benefactors—(*Dar* (Gift) of family X). Rummaging through older churches, one will find similar attestation on the bottom of chalices, on the backs of icons and on the large plaques that greet visitors to the narthex of the Church building, testifying to gifts of a by-gone era.[71] These types of special, larger gifts[72] have long had a role in Orthodox Church life, going back to the days of the Byzantine courtesans (see above). In most cases they are driven by a special, perceived, material need. Erickson's description of the collection of funds for the building of the church buildings is a similar example of this needs-driven approach.

In a similar way, Scott analyzes the psychology of giving practices and categorizes them in a way that captures a broad range of human behaviors relative to how much people give financially in the context of the parish or church.[73] He includes in this list:

a). Herd giving—the tendency of people in a new environment to follow the lead of others, usually in giving less than they would normally give so as not to stand out.

b). Comparative giving - focusing on raising the giving levels of the poorest in the group while allowing the others to give marginally despite their greater wealth.

c). Budgetary giving—this is needs-based giving as determined by a predetermined budget.

d). Averaged giving—Using simple math to divide expenses by the number of members to reach a fixed amount.

e). Legal giving: Making minimum giving a requirement—the dues system is an example. Scott notes the tendency of the minimum gift to become the normal maximum gift offered.

f). Disposable giving—basing giving on that which is left over in personal income after every other bill and expense.

It takes little analysis to see that such approaches are not based on what *God* provides, as with those who practice the 'first fruits' theology. Instead motivation for giving in these systems is based upon perceived needs or congregational dynamics. The result is often a minimalism in giving and financial shortfalls.

Rise of Ethnicism—Care of the Clan

Sociologically, one of the hidden strengths of parish life among these foundational ethnic Orthodox parishes was the parish's self-identity. It is proverbial how many of the parishioners in Orthodox parishes are related to one another (by blood) or whose families originated in the same region in Europe, the Middle East or Greece. This bonding of the Church with the local clan raised the prominence of the parish as a place where the community (clan) gathered for holidays and other important life events (i.e. baptisms, weddings, funerals). The sociological and spiritual weaknesses of the system soon became evident, however. Old World rivalries, notably among the Slavs, were transplanted into the new soil. Persons in the congregation were no longer viewed in terms of their adherence to the common Orthodox faith, but by their ethnic lineage. The parish became a welcoming community—for those who passed the tests of ethnic parish gatekeepers. Erickson states that,

> The parish became introverted, turned in upon itself, with virtually no sense of mission and outreach and with only a minimal sense of responsibility toward anyone outside its own immediate membership.[74]

In some cases, it was not even good enough for a parishioner to have come from the same Old Country as the other parishioners. Instead he also had to come from the same 'Old Village' to be *really* welcome. Such attitudes, while perhaps understandable in an Old World context, proved to be devastatingly counterproductive in America where the competitive impulses of a religious economy are at work.[75] Within a generation, many parishes began to experience declines in membership numbers (and income), due to the departure of disenfranchised members as well as the inevitable attrition resulting from those who moved from the locality to seek employment elsewhere, or became inactive due to advancing age.

The cultural introversion to which Erickson refers (including language barriers) raised serious hurdles to any new converts wishing to join the parish, even if they were drawn to Orthodoxy as their way of following Christ. Compounded with declines in the 'rust belt' economies in the decades of the 1960s, 70s and 80s, and despite the infusion of displaced persons after World War II, many parishes that were thriving communities two decades earlier were headed toward financial crisis. The gold domes of the Orthodox parishes often towered over a veritable ghost towns. The parish structures and the dues system of funding became ineffective in meeting these new demographic challenges. Those who were younger often left their home town, looking for employment. Those who did not leave were often elderly, living on fixed incomes, and unable to support the church financially with the advent of retirement. The decline of parish membership numbers often led to financial crisis.[76]

Broadly speaking, within two generations, the creative and sacrificial environment of the immigrant founders had waned or even disappeared. New, rapidly expanding and dynamic churches (usually non-Orthodox) were in a position to attract members from the established Orthodox parishes who became disgruntled with infighting. It might also be said that the local Orthodox parish could cease to be *perceived* as a worthwhile investment of human time, energy and money to those parish members who *did* remain. People would wonder out loud if there would still be a parish church from which they could be buried, after having paid their dues for generations. Insofar as American Orthodox Christians internalized these attitudes and acted upon them, they took advantage of the effectiveness of the American religious economy to provide alternatives to their personal faith life, leading to the decline of the Church of their forbears.

From Ecclesiastical Charity to Charitable Works by Societies

Lest one believe that the Orthodox Church was utterly self-absorbed, it is helpful to review briefly the work of auxiliary groups established in many parishes which provided charitable care, first to the parish community (clan) but also to the community at large. Some brotherhood and sisterhood organizations united to form national organizations to broaden the scope of their work and unite in a common cause of charity. In some cases, their efforts revolved around assisting those in the old country who remained in poverty abroad. These auxiliary organizations were often clubs, with their own membership structures that paralleled that of the church.[77] Similarly, ethnically-based fraternal organizations were formed to provide benevolence to those in need in the ethnic community, and insurance. In time, some of these organizations were effectively divorced from ecclesial roots in order to meet state insurance issuance requirements.[78]

Save for the occasional handout by the pastor to a traveler, the charitable work of the community was often carried out by the ethnic brotherhood or sisterhood, or a fraternal organization, and not necessarily identified with the *ecclesia* itself.[79] If the essential work of charity had been supplanted by an organization whose basis was not necessarily spiritual at all, but fundamentally based on ethnicity, it is doubtful that the average parish member would be led to understand the most basic elements of charity in regard to the *praxis* of the Orthodox faith as spiritual stewardship.

Stewardship and the American Orthodox Church Building

For many Orthodox immigrants who found themselves immersed in a sea of religious diversity, the appearance of an Orthodox dome on the skyline of a city or town filled with Gothic or Romanesque steeples brought a reassuring sense of self-identity. The church building was a locus of gathering, not only to worship God, but for fellowship and mutual support. It is little wonder that many Orthodox Christians today will point with pride to the church that "my father (grandfather, great grandfather) built." In such cases, the church building can become intrinsically tied to the perception of what constitutes the Church.[80] After a period of time, the feelings of good will about the church building may be replaced by angst when congregations have to consider the steep price of repairing leaky roofs, failed boilers, or retrofitting structures to accommodate an aging membership. The implications to the psychodynamics of stewardship are obvious. It is usually easier to raise funds for a new church building than to replace a boiler or a leaky roof. Many such projects involve considerable effort and expertise as well, which may be in short supply.

To anticipate these critical situations, larger churches (including most Orthodox jurisdictions) have opted to create endowment funds to 'assure' that funds are available in the future for such needs, utilizing the skills of professional fundraisers. The wisdom of such practices must be weighed carefully against the foundational principles of Orthodox Christianity, for such programs can be likened to 'storing earthly treasures' (Mt. 6:19) for a future that never arrives.[81] Scott warns, for example, about the adoption of certain non-Orthodox approaches to major fund raising:

> It is important for Orthodox Christians to understand the science of development not only because of the powerful tools it affords to the advancement of the mission of the Church but also because of the danger that the science of nonprofit institutional development presents to the church. A nonprofit organization with a cause antithetical to Orthodox teaching and life, empowered through strategic planning, emboldened by an advocating board of directors, professionally managed and adept at the challenging task of fundraising is as much a threat to the Church as militant atheism was to Orthodoxy in the twentieth century-perhaps even more so.[82]

A local parish's vision of financial stewardship in Orthodox Church life is manifest when one walks into the temple building.

Upon entering the narthex (vestibule), the faithful purchase candles to be lit in memory of loved ones as a private devotion.[83] In some cases, there are opportunities to purchase religious items, or perhaps buy items for sale as part of a current parish fund drive. Not unlike the Temple of old, many churches accommodate the purchase of sundry (primarily) religious or ethnic items in the narthex.[84] In some cases, a 'poor box' can be found, to collect funds for those in need. Given this scene however, it is questionable whether the passage of the believer through the church narthex elicits a sense of preparation for, or engagement *in his personal offering of Eucharistic thanksgiving to God*, exercised in the context of the Divine Liturgy, as may well have been the case in earlier times when the reception of offerings in the *skeuphylakion* was normative.[85]

Recent Orthodox Developments Regarding Offerings

The incorporation of the Evangelical Orthodox Church into the Antiochian Orthodox Archdiocese brought a new energy and dynamism into Orthodoxy at the end of the 20th century.[86] From the standpoint of stewardship, their impact is important because many of the converts from the Evangelical Orthodox Church (and other mission churches formed since) have brought with them a renewing spirit of sacrificial giving, including tithing, into the vocabulary and practice of Orthodoxy on a broader scale. The missionary activity springing from this watershed event has created a new dynamic in communities where startup Orthodox parishes are forming. In the language of Finke and Stark, this high cost—high reward witness to Orthodox Christianity has resulted in large numbers of persons converting to the Orthodox Church, which serves to inspire others in the mainstream of Orthodoxy to take a new look at their old faith practices.

It is not uncommon for Orthodox Christians from established parishes to relocate to a new area and join an Orthodox mission parish where the dues system and fund drive orientation has been supplanted by a personal stewardship ethic based on proportional and sacrificial giving. These new developments create new opportunities to explore and implement Orthodox stewardship in communities where the minimalism of the dues system is no longer normative. The new converts entering the Orthodox Church bring with them their existing understanding of stewardship, which, in some cases, can positively influence the *praxis* of stewardship in the local parish as a whole. However, the norms of parish life, including the practice of offering of tithes, needs to be formally grounded in an *Orthodox* understanding - in much the same way that religious education and Liturgy must be similarly grounded.

Personal Holiness and the Role of Stewardship in Orthodox America

The theoretical spiritual underpinnings of a theology of Orthodox stewardship remain present in the Orthodox Churches in America—the teachings of the Bible and Holy Tradition remain immutable. In practice, however, the models of financial giving outlined above tend to obscure and limit a fuller Orthodox *praxis* of stewardship by the faithful. Notably, the dues system created a legalistic framework for Church giving that tended to supplant the spiritual concepts of offering first fruits and abundant, sacrificial generosity. This development paralleled the emergence of a false dualism of church authority which divorced the spiritual work of the Church, and its ministry (seen to be undertaken solely by the clergy), and the care of earthly matters, which was believed to fall under the purview solely of the laity.[87]

Secondly, the vision of the parishes in the exercise of stewardship could tend to become shortsighted. Pragmatic concerns could prompt the faithful to see their donations as their offerings *to meet church needs*, with only a limited sense that Christian offerings are to be *offered to God in thanksgiving* for what *God* has given. This can lead to a false pride and vainglory (fueled by the public praise for gifts offered) that stands in contradiction to the Orthodox understanding that God Himself is the source of every good and perfect gift. Where ethnicism was forcefully present, failures of Christian charity and hospitality to non-Orthodox persons who do not share the ethnic background were inevitable. The introversion of which Erickson speaks can lead to a spiritual blindness to the requirements of hospitality. It should be noted that a type of 'reverse discrimination' against cradle Orthodox in 'convert parishes' can also arise.

Rather than being a refuge from worldliness, the parishes themselves can become tainted with a spirit of covetousness and stinginess, at times, desiring more in terms of visible, external expressions of religiosity while ignoring the call to sacrificial charity, especially to the poor. In a similar vein, fundraising schemes can be viewed as a way to get money from others, outside of the community—essentially funding the life of the Church from outside sources. Without firm ties to its fundamental spiritual roots, the dynamics of stewardship *as sacred offering* in Orthodox American parishes - both giving and distributing the offerings of the faithful - may well miss the mark.

It must be noted that in the course of these decades of Orthodox life in America, certain core elements of stewardship have remained firmly operative. Since the Divine Liturgy is the center of Orthodox stewardship, then the Church has indeed continued to celebrate in offering of that perfect sacrifice to God. The ability of the faithful to connect their personal, daily offering of their lives to the Lord, through active participation in the life of their local parish, may well have been compromised due to some of the aforementioned forces in the Religious Economy. Hence, it may be fruitful to consider ways in which the founding principles and practices of Orthodox stewardship can be re-discovered and re-implemented in this new era.

PART III

Orthodox Stewardship Today

The Tithe of Abraham
St. Sophia Seminary - South Bound Brook, NJ

CHAPTER SIX

ORTHODOX PRINCIPLES VS. ESTABLISHED PRACTICES?

Toward an Orthodox Stewardship Renewal in the Twenty-first Century

Renewal movements are common in religious economies as established churches recognize certain shortcomings of their current directions and make changes in policy or practice.[1] Such an orientation is consistent with Orthodoxy, in that the Orthodox Church believes in the presence of the Holy Spirit who guides the Church in every age and place. In this vision, renewal is always characterized by *metanoia*, a call to repentance and a change in direction or the application of life (individual or corporate) energies in the direction that leads toward the Kingdom. *Metanoia* implies an understanding that the current direction needs to be changed because it misses the mark or in some way falls short of the Way of Orthodoxy as the Way to the Kingdom. Recent works, such as those by Scott and Ferencz, help to bring a new awareness of the dynamics of leadership and stewardship issues in the Church. Through a process of sifting and discernment, Church leaders, particularly through the office of the episcopacy, can chart a path to such change.

Critical to such a path is the review of the existent structures and practices of parish and diocesan Church life that conflict with the true inner dynamics of Orthodoxy. These embedded practices may also be found to be ultimately *ineffective and detrimental* in a practical sense as well. For example, if a parish or diocesan dues system leads to a type of minimalism in offering by church members which also intrinsically countermands the Gospel norms of generosity and sacrificial *and*, (at least in certain cases) is a pragmatic failure as well, then such a system should be abandoned and replaced. A new approach is needed, that will be true to the Orthodox teaching on sacrificial giving, and based on the foundational principle that the practical needs of the Church will be met by the Lord who meets the needs of His people. Similarly, an analysis of the value and dangers of fundraising in the Orthodox parish should be reviewed in light of both spiritual and practical concerns.

In the last two decades, stewardship has become a topic of serious discussion and action within a number of Orthodox jurisdictions and programs have been developed to implement a stewardship model in parishes. Nevertheless, no single program has been so spectacularly successful as to garner broad recognition for its effectiveness in raising a broadly based spiritual awareness of the faithful about stewardship.[2] Orthodox stewardship is not a program; rather, to live Orthodox Christianity means to be a faithful steward.

Proportional Giving and the Tithe as a Pastoral Tool

Much has been said in this project about the practice of tithing and its relevance to contemporary American Orthodox Church practice. From the analysis above, it is clear that there is no specific New Testament mandate (by Christ or in the apostolic Church) to offer a tithe in a legal sense. Historically, there has been no universal canonical directive, internal law or even consistent spiritual guidance of the Church to tithe. Consequently, for the Church today to insist on the offering of a tithe by all of the faithful would be to impose a legalistic overlay on the spiritual dynamics of stewardship in Christian life.[3] Furthermore, to insist on a tithe in a legal sense might lead to a new type of minimalism, decried by Christ, where a ten percent offering could be misinterpreted as the fulfillment of God's will and satisfaction of one's responsibility in a legal sense—not unlike the present dues system. The widow's mite story reminds us of the Orthodox emphasis on the totality of generosity as the goal.

Does the tithe have a place in Orthodox Christian life? The tithe has significant value as a *pastoral aid*, in helping Christians to begin to offer and manage their financial resources received from God in a proportional, measurable, methodical and spiritually-oriented way. The calculation of one's offering in tithing begins by asking the question, "*What and how much have I received from God?*" This leads to the question, "*How can I make an offering to God in thanksgiving for what He has given me?*"[4] These are precisely the questions that can lead to a growing Christian understanding that one's offering begins *with God's gifts to us.* Assuming that a detour into legalism is avoided, tithing can serve as a starting point for developing Christian stewardship *praxis* and has immense value being part of the Law inspired by God, reflecting His beneficial guidance of human activity toward the priestly offering of the first portion of what has been received, back to Him.[5] This fosters the *Stewardship as Offering the First and Finest* dynamic, upon which this book is based, and provides an easily measurable milestone for Christians who are beginning to explore the spiritual dynamics of stewardship and offering.

Experience teaches however that the pastoral approach to teaching about practices in the Church is often more effective than any once-and-for-all edict. In this regard, *proportional giving* can be useful. Proportional giving means offering the *first and the finest* - however at first it may not be a tenth, but perhaps a lower percentage, for those who are weaker in faith or have difficulty in moving forward to the full tithe. Using this proportional giving model implies a growth process - leading from a smaller percentage to the tithe. But it also means that one is not limited to a ten percent first fruits offering, but can go beyond that to 11 percent or 15 percent or more. Again, it is based upon God's gifts to us, but also reflects sensitivity and prudent consideration of the individual's circumstance in life. In some cases, when people have resisted the full tithe as the unreasonable, the lower percentage had the benefit of opening the possibility of turning to the Lord, and trusting Him with the matter. Experience has shown that those who begin to offer even a lower percentage, even lower than a tithe, often move up the scale, to get to the tithe level sooner or later, and beyond.

From Tithing to Generosity

Like every milestone of a journey, however, the tithing marker must be passed and surpassed as the Spirit moves the soul to a deeper expression of generosity and offering of self, and what one has received, back to God. Generosity in abundance is the only true Christian standard; to settle for less is to remain in the realm of bondage to material concerns, or worse, spiritual legalism. The story of the offering of the tithe by Abba Theonas (*See Chapter IV*), and his conversion to transformative Christian generosity serves as a sound example of how sacrificial offerings of first fruits and tithes can be spiritually beneficial, while leading to true Orthodox Christian stewardship in the spirit of *abundant generosity and thanksgiving* and the totality of giving exemplified by the Widow, and indeed Christ Himself.

The teaching of sacrificial offering of a tithe of one's gross[6] income can serve as a useful, calculable starting point for this process. But to be truly Orthodox, parish members and the Orthodox parish as a whole must see stewardship in the breadth of its rightful expression—in sacrificial generosity (particularly in Eucharistic worship) and, in particular, in Christian charity.

Challenges to Progress in Personal and Parish Stewardship

The Numbers Game - Where is Everybody?

Many parishes have begun stewardship programs. Even in large parishes, much of the work of parish ministry takes place through encounters with individuals, or in very small groups. One's response to a small turnout for a stewardship study group or presentation might be discouraging to both presenter and participants.[7] This raises the question and concern - how important is the 'numbers game'? Is it really sufficient that two or three are gathered in the Lord's name for something to be effective? A presumption in the parish context is that the Spirit does indeed work where two or three are gathered. (Mt.18:20) Humanly speaking, however, it is a struggle to deal with a weak numerical response which also significantly limits the effectiveness of the emergence of a stewardship ethos in the organization. It helps immensely, however, to realize that all significant change (save for perhaps the 3000 converted on Pentecost) in the Bible happens in with 'two or three'.

Perhaps this emphasizes a little understood dimension of stewardship and ministry in general - that the long-term effectiveness of Christianity is often most often realized in small groups or steps. The Resurrection appearances of Christ, the conversion stories of Acts and other examples in scripture and Church history attest to this.

Perhaps it *must* be this way, as the individual is the one who is the steward, and the valuing of the *individual* is essential to the witness of Christianity. The questions, obstacles, and affirmations that arise in stewardship discussions are best understood as individual - even if they take place in the context of a larger group. Stewardship is intensely *personal*. The Mystery of Holy Chrismation, wherein the Orthodox Christian is 'made', emphasizes the *unique* gifts of the Holy Spirit bestowed. Every Christian is uniquely gifted, and hence uniquely *responsible* to develop those gifts and offer them to the Lord, as good and faithful steward. There are fewer events for one in pastoral ministry that bring greater joy than to see someone become aware of God's unique working in his or her life, and the joy (and awe) realizing is possible in His service as a steward of *His* gifts.

Giving based upon perceived Needs vs. what God Provides

A proportional giving model based upon <u>what God provides</u> raises an important question those who have traditionally based their giving on perceived needs. The assumption in a proportional giving /tithing model however is that *God will supply* what is needed by providing to those who are members of the community what they need for themselves and the community's needs as well. This abundance of God's gifts will overflow (in spiritual charity) to meet countless other needs in the broader community.

It is the nature of effective fundraising campaigns to foster awareness of need, and participation in the fund raising effort (event or donation campaign) to meet the need. This approach is not new, as noted above - the collection of St. Paul for the famine-afflicted churches in Palestine (2Cor.) was an example of explaining a need and creating a plan to meet it through the generosity of those who were gifted to offer. One might ask, however, about the prevalence of needs-based campaigns for Church funding on a parochial or diocesan basis. The formation of a parish budget is often based on perceived *needs* - and the parish leadership may see its role as solely trying to raise funds to meet those needs. In a proportional giving model church leaders would emphasize the community as responding to what God has *given*, and limiting expenditures accordingly. Parishes that have a solid base of proportional givers (tithes), often find that there is a surplus that allows the internal needs to be met, plus an overflow into special projects, charitable works, diocesan needs, etc.

The distinction is subtle but important. Proportional giving has a God-centered focus - the Lord will meet the needs of His people, in every way. What is offered to God by the faithful in the church offering is seen as an *responsive* offering to *God*, and hence, on a certain level, *holy*. There is an imperative to treat such offerings with a reverence for what they are - representative of the sacrifice of time, energy and love of the donors. A side benefit of this approach is that its premise serves as an antidote to superfluous, worldly spending. To live with this awareness is to invite God to direct the entire process of financial management in the church community. Needs-centered giving is, in a sense, starting from a deficit. The response is sometimes based more on the ability of someone to convince people of the 'need' than on the need itself. Marketing professionals, advertisers and some fund raisers are adept at tactics that make things seem to be a need, when they actually are not needed at all.

A distinction should be made between the church's ongoing needs and special needs. Clearly, the proportional giving model is best for addressing the former. Fundraising can be especially effective for the latter because of its motivational power, to meet limited needs (including charitable works). Many people will respond to a special call to stop the drip of an obviously leaky roof - but may be far less inclined to respond to important, but less tangible needs, like a reasonable salary for a youth minister.

Competition in Giving

Following the work of Fink and Stark, the dynamics of giving in parishes are far from immune to sociological effects. One common factor at work in social groups is *competition*. Professional fund raisers consciously (and others perhaps unconsciously) utilize this force and even manipulate it to drive giving. It was a common in the first half of the twentieth century for parish treasurers to report the offerings of the faithful in the weekly bulletin. This created some unusual dynamics (and feelings) in the congregation. For some, it was a point of pride (or vainglory) and there was a 'price' to pay if one's donation was not listed.[8] The wealthy were expected to give more - and the report would list whether they were giving their fair share. It would also indicate who gave nothing, or was behind on their 'obligation'. In other cases, listing donations was done to prompt others to also give and to 'match' the giving level of their friends. This sword is double edged however, since some might be prompted to keep levels artificially low because everyone else was giving at that level.

This method of fund raising is often used in social settings and fund raising dinners. It is sometimes prompted by emotion - seeing a need met through charitable action, or the witness of the response of another person walking up and making a donation publicly.

Of course, the biblical injunctions of Christ concerning the Widow's Mite and one's "right hand not knowing what your left hand is doing" (Mt. 6:3) speaks to the dangers of these methods. They may be effective to some degree, but based on emotion they are not sustainable long term. If they foster vainglory, they are not virtuous but self-serving.

Mixed Messages—Parish Dues

Many parishes in various Orthodox jurisdictions were historically based on the Congregationalist model and funded significantly by annual dues.[9] Decades of practice have embedded the dues structure in the minds of the faithful as 'normal'. For such cradle Orthodox, both clergy and laity, the notion of changing the system in their parish (even if it would be required for their very survival) may present itself to be quite a radical change. For parishes where the practice is anonymous giving, it may lead to confusion if parish members begin to read donation amounts in their diocesan newspapers.

The parish dues system is one reflection of a deep chasm between an Orthodox understanding of stewardship and Church authority and its *praxis* as lived in many parishes and diocesan structures. If our stewardship mirrors our relationship with God and our world view, the practice of financial management based on a system of minimal parish dues will have implications about spiritual matters that are not intended and are inconsistent with the whole of Orthodox Christianity.

Making the Shift - Parish Stewardship Programs

To make the shift from a dues-based parochial structure to a proportional giving model is no small task. It cannot be accomplished en masse, through authoritarian edict or over a short time frame. To accomplish such a shift would require at least:

- A structural means of dissemination of information through presentations and literature that could introduce Orthodox stewardship through proportional, sacrificial giving as a 'new normal.'

- Parish leadership - lay and clergy - need to be committed to the transformation process. These leaders may need to wrestle with both the structural and behavioral issues raised by such a change, perhaps even changes to the parish constitution.

The spiritual and teaching roles of the pastor cannot be underestimated in this scenario.

- An outside speaker or consultant might be effective in presenting concepts, answering questions and providing support, but ultimately the parish would have to entrust the process to God, for His inspiration to change minds and hearts. It is not enough to simply give presentations or materials, but a process of an extended dialogue is needed to allow questions to be fully addressed and for confidence to build. There is something to be said, however, for the 'outside expert' who sometimes comes across as more credible than those in the community who may be saying the same things.

One of the most effective means to bring a tangible awareness of what Orthodox stewardship is about can be found in *remembering*, not only the practices of the ancient past, but of a parish's own history. In the United States almost every parish has powerful stories of how its founders made great sacrifices - financially and personally - so that the Church would come into existence locally, that its visible symbol (the temple) would be constructed, and that it would be supported financially, especially in the most difficult times.[10]

Given all of these challenges, is it possible to make progress in parish stewardship *praxis* through a parish stewardship program? *Such an effort would be as worthwhile as it is necessary.* Even if large numbers of people did not participate at first, those who *did* benefit from such an effort could serve as a leaven and witness to the whole community, as they grow personally by living lives of sacrificial giving and generosity. In the best of circumstances, no parish educational effort is universally successful. Instead, what the Church always does is present the Gospel; some will accept it unto spiritual growth and life, while others will reject it. The presentation of the principles of a God-centered process of sacrificial giving would help to offer an alternative focus for financial life in the parish which is different from the needs-driven, fundraising orientation that is common.

Challenging Presumptions or Worldviews.

Like all Orthodox Christian religious formation, stewardship education is more about changing a world view and practice than merely providing information or data about the Bible or Church history. It is one thing to expose the assumptions of one's world view; it is quite another thing to teach people persuasively that the Orthodox way, as presented from its biblical and theological roots, is preferable, possible and even *necessary*. Key to the success of this process is providing effective tools to put the stewardship practices into practice

Some will not 'get the message' that to be an Orthodox Christian means living a sacrificial lifestyle. There may always be a temptation to offload the responsibility for funding the parish to others, including outsiders. This is one of the great dangers to the parishes that base a significant percentage of their income on fundraisers.

It should be noted, given all that has been said about stewardship as offering to God, that Orthodox stewardship has very little in common with certain atheistic, materialistic, agnostic or neo-pagan philosophies present today that do not begin with a sense of the primacy of God as Lord, and our relationship to Him guiding our view of the cosmos in light of that revelation. Many people of good will today use the term 'stewardship' in a variety of social and economic contexts, without such a basis. Care should be taken to realize that when the Christians engage with others in such stewardship discussions, that this difference in perspective may well radically change the means and direction of 'stewardship' activities. In the worst case, arguments can be made for totalitarianism and political solutions as a means of 'stewardship' of world resources which are little more than thinly veiled egoistic/nationalistic attempts at power and manipulation. Such may well be opposed to the Orthodox stewardship principles that emphasize freedom, selflessness, generosity and responsibility.

Facing the Challenges—Stewardship Education

In first attempting to address this issue, it became clear that there is a dearth of written Orthodox material on the subject of stewardship in English. Save for the works by Scott (*Good and Faithful Steward*), Wesche (*The Theology of Stewardship in Light of Orthodox Tradition*) and several articles, including shorter articles within other books, I was unable to find much extensive theological writing on the topic in print on the subject in English.[11] This may imply that the Orthodox Church sees stewardship more as a part of a greater whole of Christian life, than a topic unto itself. Orthodox stewardship must be illuminated not only by its biblical roots, but by other dimensions of Holy Tradition as well, so that it is not simply an appendage (albeit interesting) to Christian life, but a component part.

As the understanding of the ancient Orthodox practice of stewardship emerges, it is impossible to implement if there is no broad-based understanding of its Source, its challenges, and spiritual benefits. While written and electronic media can be made available to people, a more powerful example often emerges when people share their stories - recounting how God has blessed them, their fears and reservations about their response as stewards, and their offering to God the first and finest of all that He has bestowed.

One challenge in any catechetical endeavor is customizing the content for a specific audience. Among the groups that can, and should be addressed in such catechetical efforts include:

Clergy Leaders - Coursework and presentations in seminaries and continuing education for clergy can be helpful both for the clergy themselves and their ministry. The clergy can only lead effectively in this area if they themselves and their families are growing in their stewardship awareness and practice.

Lay Leadership Development - Lay leadership in parishes and in jurisdictional leadership bodies play a powerful role through both decision-making, and perhaps more importantly, their personal witness to Christian life. If lay leaders exemplify a sound Christian approach to stewardship - not only financially but in other aspects of life - it will permeate the *ethos* of the parish. The same can be said of the personal practice of the pastor and his family.

Youth Ministry and Church School - provide the opportunity to form a future generation of faithful stewards in the parish. Creative efforts to make Orthodox stewardship understandable at an early age can be very effective in the long term. Orthodoxy has an advantage because of its bodily activities - hence the notion of *offering* can be embodied in a variety of creative activities for youth. Stewardship education in church camps and vacation school programs provides special opportunities to address stewardship thematically.

Senior Citizens - often face extraordinary challenges in life, but perhaps are best able to see the spiritual implications of a total consecration of life to God, at the heart of Orthodox stewardship. The encounter with suffering and death can be sobering, but for those who are prepared, the long-awaited moment of the eternal reward to the good and faithful servant can bring to sharp focus the energies of one's Christian life. The matter of the disposition of one's estate raises important stewardship questions in almost every case.

Converts - As mentioned above, the zeal of new converts to Orthodoxy can be positive force for growth in the parish. New converts need an Orthodox understanding of proportional giving/tithing as a form a financial offering and stewardship. This must be linked to their emerging understanding all things Orthodox, including the theology, liturgy, morality and ecclesiology. Stewardship actually serves as a helpful framework to address many other topics in Church life. In some cases, as with personal theologies or practices, these must be channeled into an Orthodox understanding and practice.

Families - The implications of the stewardship mindset can have a profound effect when addressed on the family level. When parents see their roles in childrearing as *caretakers* of their children, entrusted to them by God, they are challenged to a faith-based approach to child rearing. Such realizations inform many dimensions of life - spiritual practices, liturgy participation, support for the parish, family financial management, etc. The opportunities for formation in these areas are extensive.

Orthodox Media - The existing Orthodox media (including print, audio and Internet) can be utilized for Orthodox stewardship education efforts. Ancient Faith Radio (ancientfaith.com), the Orthodox Christian Network (myocn.net), and The Orthodox Steward (orthodoxsteward.com) offer electronic information and media on Orthodox stewardship. However, there is no substitute for person-to-person interactions wherein "two or three gathered" experience the presence of the risen Lord and enter into an understanding of His teaching in the heart.

From the study of early Church practices (see Chapter 4) it would appear that there is a *great* wealth of primary source material that can inform our contemporary understanding of Orthodox stewardship, but much work remains for Orthodox scholars to accomplish in this area.[12] Of particular importance for the Orthodox Church are the relationships between stewardship and offering (particularly in the Liturgy) and the role of personal and corporate charity as key to the practice of Christian stewardship. The wealth of the Scriptures and Tradition should be mined to bring forth the treasure of these sources to inform the conscience of Christians and the Church as a whole. A critique of non-Orthodox[13] practices and approaches would also be helpful. From such a study could emerge a sound teaching series, homily resources, financial management 'best practices' directives and other helpful materials for use on the parish level.

Principles for Emphasis in Stewardship Programs

From the analysis above, the following principles of Orthodox stewardship are highlighted as foundational concepts for an understanding of Orthodox Stewardship.

1. **Spiritual offering to God in thanksgiving is the basis of stewardship in Orthodoxy.** The summit of our spiritual offering is the offering of the Eucharistic Liturgy. Key to this understanding is the realization by Orthodox Christians that their eternal relationship with God as well as their day-to-day life experiences and material wealth *can be offered in thanksgiving to God*—spiritually and tangibly, in a representative fashion, in the ecclesial Eucharistic. This is the fulfillment of the priestly vocation of men and women, leading to communion with God and *theosis*.

Failure to psychologically connect one's personal offerings and financial management to this spiritual core of Orthodoxy may lead to a dualistic mindset: material *vs.* spiritual, lay *vs.* clergy, church *vs.* world, practical *vs.* mystical.[14]

2. **Firstfruits offering and Proportional Giving play a key role in Orthodox stewardship practice.** Although there is *some* evidence in Church Tradition of a practice of financial offering of a fixed percentage of income (tithing), there is no evidence that it was established as a widespread *norm* of Orthodox practice in the first millennium; it would be an innovation to insist on such in the Church today.[15] Rather than being a legalistic requirement or spiritual directive, the offering of a tithe may be better seen as a type of image (icon) of the virtuous offering of first fruits in thanksgiving for the gifts that God has bestowed upon us.

In many contexts, including practical and spiritual interpretations, the offering of firstfruits *has* been a consistent theme in the Orthodox spiritual tradition. The Church continues to uphold the higher Christian standard, taught and sacrificially offered by Christ on the Cross and exemplified by the holy martyrs and saints, which encourages the faithful to a *total* consecration of self and wealth in following Christ. As a spiritual process toward sanctity (*theosis*), this total offering is not made at once, but rather through a series of many smaller personal offerings (willful acts of consecration) made along the road of life leading to this fuller, total offering as realized totally in death - the death to self in Christ. Offering of a tithe of ten percent of gross income may be a helpful step for someone on this path to holiness.

3. **Sound, courageous, stewardship programs will challenge the status quo of flawed Church structures and practices**. Among the issues for consideration would be a review of the fundamental roles of lay and clergy leaders and the shortcomings of common lay Parish Board (vs. episcopal/clerical leadership) structures and the membership dues systems. Pastoral prudence is necessary in such cases, where embedded practices are sometimes 'enshrined' and without a strong catechesis beforehand, upsetting the status quo may cause serious disruption on many levels in parish life. In communities where parish life is self-oriented, a new outward looking orientation will need to be presented.

4. **Orthodox Stewardship will be exemplified by service to the local poor, both individually and communally, and further by service beyond the local community.** When the Church manifests the love of Christ to those in need, the parish itself is immersed in the saving love of Christ. Part of this vision is the recovery of the expression of the *corporate* stewardship role of the parish as the primary and central locus of Orthodox Christian charity. Historically, the diaconate was a key element of this dimension of stewardship.[16] In some cases this orientation toward service will be new, and in other cases a renewal or re-energizing of existing charitable efforts.

5. **A stewardship emphasis brings the 'other-worldly' eschatological vision of Orthodoxy into day-to-day parish life, enabling Orthodox Christians to combat the pervasive pragmatism, sensuality and materialism of the age.** Orthodox stewardship begins with a radical affirmation

that 'God is the Lord' and Provider of 'every good and perfect gift'. This world view not only lies in direct opposition to cultural materialism (idolatry) of our age, but serves as way to combat it. Not only is such a vision fundamental to Orthodox life and liturgy, it is also conducive to Church growth, as noted by Finke and Stark.[17] An Orthodox stewardship orientation becomes a beacon of saving grace in a world darkened by materialism and godless secularism. This vision makes gives human beings to their true human (not merely religious) vocation - to be *priest*, who offers to God first, and does not focus all of his energies or resources on himself.

6. **Parishioners can experience new insights into other dimensions of Orthodox spiritual life through stewardship study.** Stewardship is not a separate component of parish life divorced from the rest (liturgy, social activity, fellowship and parish harmony, leadership meetings, etc.) Rather, the internal attitudes of the parish concerning stewardship are reflective of a broader patterns of Orthodox parish life that is based *either in the principles of the Gospel, or those of the world.* Hence, practical problems which are found to exist in parish life may have their roots in issues related to stewardship, or they may at least be informed by the spiritual principles of Orthodox stewardship.[18] For individuals, moral teachings can often be seen more clearly through the lens of stewardship - moral life being a means of consecration of oneself to God. The liturgical services can be understood as an active, prayerful *offering* by *all*, engaging people to participate in worship in a more focused, and meaningful way. The call to service as faithful stewardship may lead people to a deeper spiritual life of service to the parish community in myriad ways, or to the poor.

Toward Institutional Renewal

While the personal practice and witness is essential to an Orthodox ethos of stewardship, the systemic problems with church structures and practices rooted in un-Orthodox and non-Christian practices will be a stumbling block to a penetration of a stewardship mindset into church structures. In locations (diocesan or parochial) where these structures are embedded, a comprehensive approach by leaders (lay and clergy) must be channeled to propose alternatives and teach. The role of the hierarchs in this matter cannot be underestimated, as their office as stewards/overseers of the entire Church. Perhaps, one cannot replace a failed structure until there is an interim structure in place, until a solid, sound new structure can be implemented without unintended harm. This analogy means that processes of change in the Church need to be thoughtful, sensitive, well-planned and led with strength.

Parish Administration—Trust in God, Personal Faith

As an outgrowth of this project, it has become clear that Orthodox stewardship must be formed in a vision of the Providence of God,[19] the Giver of every good and perfect gift.[20] All that is in human existence owes itself to Him. In Orthodoxy, the priestly movement in the human soul (in freedom) responding to God in His goodness, and the offering, in return, one's own gifts with thanksgiving, form an essential dimension of the Divine-human interchange.

These two essential elements serve as starting point for a fuller understanding of the many dimensions of that which we call 'stewardship'. An approach to stewardship (or Church financial matters) that does not begin with these basic tenets will miss the mark. Church administration not fostered in the correct spirit will inevitably lead to a 'fallen' way of operation. The temptations to personal sin may well translate into *institutional* sins (embedded in policy and practice) - resulting in institutional greed, sloth, presumption, or pride - rather than Christian virtues.[21]

Parish structures where a vibrant stewardship model is in place will invariably give witness to the priorities as embodied in the teachings of Christ. In such a parish, the faithful will be reminded of their participatory role in offering as part of their worship, in the necessity of offering worthy first fruits, and in generosity and charity toward those in need. To the extent that these practices are embedded in the very structures of parish life, they will cease to be invisible, but will, instead, lead to a conscious movement in the minds and souls of participants leading to engagement in the sacrificial worship of the Liturgy and the practice of charity toward those in need.[22]

Financial and Material Wealth in the Church

It is an ongoing temptation to see the acquisition of wealth or facilities of the Church as an end in itself.[23] Stewardship implies that the Church building and resources must serve the greater plan of the Master. Jesus repeatedly reminded his followers that His Kingdom was not of this world and that even the Temple would be destroyed. If a desire for temporal goods infiltrates the mindset of the parish (or its leadership) the parish may be tempted to seek money as an end in itself.[24] A second temptation is to seek financial gain and pay parish bills in ways that are inappropriate for Christian communities, regardless of how effective they might be. Fundraising schemes that impoverish others or weigh on their personal weaknesses or passions would, in most cases, fall in this category.[25] Similarly, the desire for material goods can also lead to unwise indebtedness, the burden of which can rob a parish of its spiritual vitality. This consideration becomes particularly important as a Church purchases property (invariably with a substantial mortgage) or does major facility upgrades or renovations.

The contemporary American Orthodox Church ethos is not egalitarian, nor has it ever been.[26] Some persons are entrusted with more wealth by God and shall be called to account for it at the Final Judgment. The Church has a responsibility to teach and minister to all persons about financial stewardship—the poor and the wealthy as well. A successful, broad-based stewardship initiative of teaching and formation throughout the parish might tend to elicit a higher donation level from more people, tending to shift the dependency of the parish financially away from a wealthy individual or individuals. However, this shift will never eliminate the trend where the majority of the wealth in the parish tends to come from those who are wealthy. This is both a spiritual and a mathematical reality which must be acknowledged. In fact, when cognizant of the dangers mentioned above, it is a good thing when the wealthy respond through giving; if the numbers are skewed, so be it.

Stewardship as Charity to the Poor

As a whole, much of our concern today with financial stewardship is focused on the role of individuals and practical parish needs met through financial offerings that are usually applied to sustain the parish. Yet the fact that patristic sources refer primarily to the role of charity to the poor and almsgiving should serve as an essential pillar in our modern view of Christian stewardship as well. If any conclusion can be drawn, it is that much, much more work needs to be done in this area.[27] The history of the Church is replete with examples of Church renewal through charitable work. Charity is simply stewardship offering to God by ministering to his servants, the poor. The *encouragement* afforded to the Church (and the world) when the Church exercises self-disinterested charity is unmistakable. In the early Church, the exercise of charity was often a powerful witness to the pagans to a truth incomprehensible in human terms, God's love manifest through the true nature of Christianity.[28] The establishment and nurturing of ecclesial structures, policies and ministries is clearly in fulfillment of this goal.

The generosity of the great saints of Orthodoxy who gave alms and extended extraordinary charity to the poor serves as a living example to the contemporary Church of the importance of charity and generosity to those in need.[29] Such an outpouring would bring relief of suffering and the mercy of God to those in need, and a spiritual transformation in the hearts of believers and non-believers alike. Orthodox communities should take the lead by making charitable giving a keystone to their community life, thereby giving witness to the charity of Christ in the world. *This is what it means to be the Church of Jesus Christ.* Sacrificial generosity means that the needs of the poor are not overlooked, even when the parish has its own financial responsibilities and burdens, but rather charity is firmly established as a priority in the parish hierarchy of values and that sacrificial giving is required to meet the both sets of priorities.

There are secondary benefits realized by the parish community when engaged in charitable work. When the community exercises Christian charity to those in need as a dimension of parochial stewardship, an extraordinary energy and dynamism becomes palpable in the community itself. Many pastors can recall experiences when parish members have extended themselves by working on special charity projects, overseas missions, soup kitchens, prison ministry and the like. They often return with joy and renewed commitment to living the Faith. They experience an emerging understanding of the teachings of Christ in a way that transcends the intellect and it enlivens the soul. This is the recognition that stewardship *as ministry*, and empowered by the Holy Spirit, to bring forth the love of Christ into the world—a cause for great joy.[30] Frequently, when parish members are engaged in dynamic charitable service, the parish as a whole participates in these efforts by sharing its financial resources, and shares in the joy as well.

The value of establishing parish administrative structures to maintain effective, ongoing charitable work should not be underestimated. Charity committees, food pantries, volunteer pools, emergency response teams and similar activity groups serve as an *ongoing* witness to the entire parish of the dedication of the Church expressed locally to stewardship through charity. Such groups provide a necessary framework that promotes these charitable efforts. When such structures are weak or absent, the witness to the parish's commitment to the exercise of stewardship through charity may wane or collapse entirely.

<u>Stewardship in Established Parishes</u>

The original exploration of stewardship for the doctoral project which spawned this book dealt with mission parishes, but a number of clergy who serve established parishes have asked questions about the degree to which these mission parish stewardship approaches might be extended into an established parish context. At first glance, the dynamics appear to differ significantly. However, if the premise is true that Christian stewardship *as offering the first and finest* is a fundamental element of Orthodox Christian life, then should be applicable in all contexts.

Lessons need to be learned when stewardship efforts fail or fall short in the local context. Such situations create financial stress on parishes that can be harmful if not devastating. For example, if financial oversight in the parish is weak and funds are found to be stolen or used foolishly, the effect is not only financial, but spiritual. Fundamental trust in the parish is weakened or even destroyed.

This is no small matter, first and foremost because the judgment of God begins with the household of faith (1Pt. 4:17). The punishment of the unfaithful steward (individual or corporate) who has been entrusted with great treasures (spiritual and material) will be both swift and thorough (Mt. 25:14ff). The divisive internal forces that arise when financial worries predominate in the minds and hearts of parish members can result in a rupture in the fellowship of a church community. Spiritual disunity born of poor stewardship may result from ignorance of the importance of financial stewardship in the first place. The founding members of a parish may have known of the importance of sacrificial giving, but their grandchildren may not. Hence it is incumbent on clergy to bring the fullness of the Christian gospel to the community regarding sacrificial (Christ-like) giving which will lead to deeper commitment and unity in the Body.

In addition, the authenticity of the apostolic witness of the Gospel by the Church in the world depends not only upon the effective presentation of the teachings of the Christ to non-believers, but as much (or more so) upon the spiritual witness of faith communities living in the Spirit according to that teaching. When individuals (clergy or laity), parishes, or whole churches miss the mark (sin) in their personal or corporate stewardship of God's gifts, the effectiveness of the Church in engaging the world with the Gospel will be thwarted and the spiritual battle will go badly.[31] I believe that financial stewardship is the 'front line' of that battle in our American culture today.

When the hearts and minds of God's people in the parish are exposed to the teachings of the Gospel, the light of the Holy Spirit will bring insight which can lead to a change in the heart (*metanoia*) where needed. That Jesus Himself so often used financial stewardship in describing the way to holiness, through His teachings, parables and examples (see Section II), means that His Church should be keenly aware of how these dynamics play out in the lives of the Christian faithful. The examples of Christians giving generously can be a very powerful force for renewal.

Stewardship in Mission Parishes

A strategy of teaching and formation of Orthodox Christians in the area of stewardship is *essential* in Orthodox life in all parishes, but perhaps more so in newly formed parishes in the United States. While this may tend be addressed as a dollar-cents reality check in mission parishes, the fostering of the underlying spiritual dynamic of stewardship is a real key to the kind of spirit of thanksgiving, faith, hospitality and sharing that makes mission parishes vibrant.

The growth of mission parishes will hinge on the community's capacity to offer their support of time, energy, talent, and faith to the process. Founding a mission parish assumes a dedicated core of individuals who are willing to offer their personal resources to the growth of the church, sacrificially. At every step of growth of the mission: holding services, evangelistic outreach, formation of administrative structures, planning, purchasing property, financial management/church loans, etc. all have a stewardship component. If this component is both strong from the beginning and spiritually oriented the mission parish character will be Christian, if not, it will be something else.

In missions, where a stewardship ethic is firmly operative, the generous sharing of God's gifts will be manifest in two distinct realms— the sharing of the Gospel through the establishment of the new mission community, and the generous sharing of financial treasures with the poor.[32] These are powerful forces in the witness to Orthodox Christianity present from the apostolic age, and the Spirit of God confirms these human activities prompted by divine grace. This stewardship *ethos* can be a font of spiritual life and even renewal for the *whole* Church. The broader Church often sees its true calling when mission work is present dynamically, as in Acts of the Apostles. This serves both as an encouragement, and a challenge, to rally more resources (through sacrificial giving of every type) to work synergistically with the Holy Spirit in this salvific work.

An Outpouring of Grace

As noted at the beginning, the thrust of this work has focused on financial stewardship and offering. Yet God has bestowed a multitude of gifts upon humankind. The most profound, of course, is the relationship with God Himself, afforded through our creation in His image and likeness, restored through the Incarnation of the Divine Son of God and His saving Paschal Mystery, and enlivened through the Gift of Gifts, the Holy Spirit Himself. Compared to these spiritual realities, the gift of earthly treasure takes its rightful place, rather low on the priority of things, yet remains a real, tangible gift and sign of God's love, care and providence.

Every human relationship, including those in the Church, are a gift of God's loving grace - and the experience of the loss of a loved one reminds us of how precious those relationships are. Often our gifts are best appreciated when they are seemingly absent. The gift of children is recognized profoundly by the childless couple praying for a child. The gift of health is appreciated when the doctor informs us that our death may be sooner than we realized. The gift of our home is missed terribly when a tragic fire takes it away. Notably, Orthodox theologians are addressing dimensions of Christian stewardship and ecology, as well as systemic problems of poverty in the world.[33]

Most of the gifts of greatest worth are intangible. Who has immigrated to the United States from an oppressive homeland and not been struck by the gift of freedom afforded us in our society? The gift of love - of a spouse, of a child, of a faithful friend may ebb or flow from ones consciousness, but it is a gift that is entrusted to us, by God and life-giving.

Orthodox Stewardship calls us to be caretakers of all of these gifts. This requires a sensitivity and receptivity to the gift, in the Christian understanding. It becomes obvious that stewardship extends far beyond the realm of material treasure, into every aspect of life. To the traditional list of time, talent and treasure should be added the gift of **trust** - that intangible but essential element of human relationships that makes all human social life, commerce and love possible.

CHAPTER SEVEN

MODELS AND RESOURCES FOR ORTHODOX PARISH STEWARDSHIP PROGRAMS

Programs of Stewardship Development in Orthodox Jurisdictions in the United States

The Orthodox jurisdictions in the United States have been developing stewardship programs for parish use for over two decades. The impetus for this development has waxed and waned over the years. For the most part, these programs are spiritually oriented, with the desire to develop a model of stewardship that reflects the Gospel principles of sacrificial offering. In other cases the focus has been more pragmatic - based upon a desire to replace outmoded dues systems and overstretched fund raising schemes that can no longer sustain parish financial operations. These programs have invoked the Gospel principles elucidated herein, but certain elements have not necessarily been emphasized.

The Greek Orthodox Archdiocese (GOA) has produced programs in annually for over 15 years that have promoted a commitment to stewardship, and identified a component of parish membership connected with one's pledge of a financial offering made in the course of the stewardship promotion. Typically this process has had a kick off on a given Sunday in the fall, when all parishes are to hold a Stewardship Sunday program, and the materials for the in-parish stewardship homilies and lay presentations are thematically developed by the Archdiocese and forwarded to the parish for this purpose.

However, the Stewardship Ministry office has emphasized that the Stewardship program is designed to be ongoing effort on the parish level. One key is the formation of a special stewardship committee that works in conjunction with the parish board and pastor to promote stewardship throughout the process. Communication with members and small group discussions with the Stewardship Committee are also encouraged and resources (including a video) are provided. A Stewardship Commitment Card helps members to tangibly commit to the stewardship process and other creative print and media materials are also available for existing and new parish members.

In addition, in the Greek Archdiocese, development related programs are also implemented by the Archdiocesan Council Stewardship Committee which has subcommittees to promote planned giving, estate planning and other financial stewardship resources. A national stewardship training opportunity is also offered by the national Stewardship Committee to provide local training in parishes and groups. Key to any such programmatic development is a substantial base of committed and trained leaders and funding to develop and disseminate the message of stewardship from the central Church organization to the parishes.

The Orthodox Church of America (OCA) has had programs in place for several decades as well. The OCA website has a Stewardship Resource[1] with a discussion of "Moving from a Dues System to Stewardship" with a sample pledge card. This card suggests a 3% offering as a starting point if the 10% tithe is not possible. There are a limited number of other articles listed on the website addressing stewardship topics, but some are rather dated.

The Antiochian Archdiocese made a move toward a 'proportional giving' model in 2006 but set in place a rather complex system of assessment and 'Special Tray' offerings made by the parishes to the Archdiocesan center. On the parish level a '52 Week Parish Giving Program'[2] serves as a resource to help promote stewardship year-round, emphasizing that it is based *strictly on scriptural and church teachings and not on the parish's financial condition.* The Antiochian program attempts to address the thorny issues of parish membership and giving - delineating differences between 'Voting members' and 'Members in good standing' and tying certain stewardship behaviors to the latter. Such a program would require amendment to the parish's constitution (based upon the diocesan Model Constitution). The 52 Week Program delineates specifically between a tithe (10%) and offerings, the latter always being defined as above and beyond the basic tithe.[3] The program delineates a five week letter campaign accompanied by homilies on Sundays that emphasize stewardship themes, and their relationship of stewardship to practical parish matters, like the budget. The program also encourages group and individual visitations and small group discussions. The program also notes biblical and patristic background resources for use throughout the fifty two weeks of the year. The Antiochian Church also has a Parish Council Handbook that delineates specifics about how stewardship should be implemented on a parish level.

In a similar manner, the Serbian Orthodox jurisdiction in North and South America has a comprehensive program developed annually for use in the parishes, including homilies and lists of persons available to speak to stewardship themes locally. The Carpatho-Russian diocese has a Stewardship Commission that is developing a series of resources, stewardship programs and travelling presentations to raise stewardship awareness. Other jurisdictions have resources available as well, and in some cases, more formal programs.

Proposed Parish Program - UOC of USA

Appendix I outlines a program which was originally established for use by the Ukrainian Orthodox Church of the USA. While implemented in only a limited number of contexts, the program focuses on the principles of spiritual offering as the basis of Orthodox Stewardship. It recognizes the importance of a long-term, intentional educational process upstream of pledge drives and the like, to better lay a foundation for spiritual understanding and approach to the stewardship responsibility. It also draws upon the spiritual tradition of Ukrainian Orthodoxy, particularly the tithe of St. Volodymyr, as a model for Orthodox stewardship today.

Pledging Programs

One key element to most parish stewardship programs is the commitment action made by individual members in their conscience and expressed tangibly through a signed commitment or pledge card. In most cases this pledge is represented as a percentage of income (sometimes adjusted to personal circumstances) and in other cases a fixed dollar amount. Each has its advantages. The former is to be preferred because it represents proportional giving, and bases the actual amount offered upon God's blessings received. It is an opportunity to see God as the source of personal funds. The latter offers the advantage of giving parish council or finance committee planners a fixed amount from which they can anticipate receiving when forming a budget. Some parishes have promoted pledging precisely for this reason - dividing the expected parish expense budget by the number of giving units and mandating this as an expected 'pledge'. If coercive, such a process can compromise parish social dynamics by making the financial outlay a hardship on some. In addition, it has been argued that a pledge may actually have *legal* implications, and legally binding upon those making pledge.[4]

One advantage of having pledge drives is that the emotional and sociological effects of joint participation in giving can be a very positive influence in the parish. When others see the parish leaders pledging their personal resources they can be inspired to join in the effort. The tangible pledge promotes that process. The downside of pledge programs is that they can become simply a new routine for the parish. People think, "It's pledge time." Perhaps if they see such a notice in the Parish Bulletin, they may decide to take the Sunday off because they may believe heard it all before. The effectiveness of any such drive lies in its ability to form a spiritual Orthodox mindset about offering - what it can accomplish and the mission of the Church - which brings joy and engages the parishioners actively.

> *Note that there is a multitude of resources available from Orthodox jurisdictions elsewhere in addition to Protestant, Roman Catholic and secular resources in print and online. The bibliography below may also be helpful for further reading, however all these resources have not been cannot be compiled here, and it can be assumed that non-Orthodox sources will not come from the same premise that Stewardship begins with sacred offering - the premise of this writing.*

FINAL THOUGHTS

Worship of the Angels
Adapted from the work of Winnie Pizzitola, Iconographer

As Orthodox Christians, our participation in the offering of the Divine Liturgy is the central moment in our lives when God receives *us - in union with His Son, Jesus Christ* as a sacred gift offered by Christ, the High Priest. This offering of our selves, joined to crucified and risen Christ in the Eucharist, is the perfect and acceptable sacrifice; it reveals to humankind the Lordship of God over all, and offers to us the opportunity to fulfill our human vocation as priest through His priestly offering. The wise exercise of faithful and charitable stewardship of God's gifts, by Christians and by His Church, will be a sign of the Kingdom, and lead to the salvation of souls who make such a sacred offering. As the Eucharist is Christ's offering - "Thine own of Thine own", it represents the *first and finest* of all that is fully human in its spiritual and material existence as redeemed in Christ. In this action, the process of *theosis* is realized - a communion of our humanity with God. This is recognized not simply individually, but when the Church gathers as the *synaxis* of believers, joined by the angels and saints, who corporately make this offering liturgically and through ministry to the world. This is the stewardship of the Church in the world.

This dynamic of *offering* underlies all that is truly human and being central to the Orthodox faith draws the discussion of stewardship to all of the core elements of all that is Orthodox. The Liturgy and its texts becomes not only a font of understanding about how the acceptable Eucharistic offering is made, but becomes the very means through which we make the offering. The Holy Scriptures, reflecting the infinite condescension and offering of Christ in the Incarnation and the sacrificial offering unto death on the Cross, reveals how humanity is joined by divine grace and love to the acceptable offering of Christ to the Father and has inspired the Christian faithful, especially the holy martyrs, to reveal to all mankind the true stewardship of *human life* through offering. Holy Tradition, as the lived experience of the Church as led by the Holy Spirit, reveals countless insights into how the way of stewardship as offering has been manifest, through the teaching and examples of the Holy Fathers, the iconographic tradition, the holy canons, the liturgical life, and other dimensions of lived Orthodoxy in time and place.

The sacrificial nature of Christianity implies that we offer our *first and finest* to the Lord. From this initial offering flows a spiritual capacity to enable the faithful stewardship of the entirety of our lives - our human relationships, our material wellbeing, our spiritual gifts and human capabilities - carried out in a holy manner pleasing to God in the *ongoing liturgy* which is human life. Generous offering to the poor becomes more than a moral dictum, but becomes a participation in this offering dynamic to Christ who is embodied in the poor and accepts the material offerings of those who so offer in love.

The theoretical teachings of the Church regarding stewardship, the witness of generous Christian people and the daily challenges of overcoming my own spiritual shortcomings (personally and in ministry) through the course of this stewardship study have made me aware of the importance of sacrificial *kenosis* in Christ (Phil. 2:4) at the heart of Christian stewardship. Ours is a call to offer the *first and finest* of all entrusted to us. In doing so, may we become the good and faithful stewards that Christ calls each of us to be. This requires us to acquire the mind of Christ and become a living sacrifice—a lifelong process of selflessness stewardship - offering nothing less than the *first and finest* of ourselves and all that we have from Him, in Eucharistic thanksgiving.

APPENDIX

A SAMPLE PARISH STEWARDSHIP PROGRAM

Below is a blueprint for a parish stewardship program originally prepared for use by parishes of the Ukrainian Orthodox Church of U.SA. It can be adapted to parish needs, regardless of size, ethnic composition, history, etc. For more information, contact the Office of Stewardship, Ukrainian Orthodox Church of the USA: stewardship@uocusa.net

1. **Initial Discussion:** A visit and presentation is made to the *parish leadership* by the Stewardship Director about stewardship in general, as well as what is involved in going from a traditional dues/fundraising model of parish finances to a stewardship model. <u>It is essential that the pastor and lay leaders be active participants in the subsequent parish stewardship activities.</u>

2. **Stewardship Information Phase:** This is an extended period during which the parish receives information from a variety of sources about the nature of Christian stewardship. An extensive list of print and media materials, including a video series of Stewardship presentations on DVD, will be made available to parishes that enroll in this process. The goal is broad-based information for all parish members to gain a familiarity and understanding of what Orthodox stewardship is, and is not. The materials are presented and discussed in a way that is effective for each parish - adult education, parish sermons, reading groups, coffee hour presentations, etc.

3. **Leadership Discernment Phase:** Parish leaders, including clergy and laity, determine whether a transition to a proportional giving - stewardship model is desirable and timely.

Leaders must determine what impediments exist within the parish membership and structures that might undermine this significant shift in the way the parish carries out its mission. If, leaders determine that such a transition is feasible and desirable, they are trained to understand and explain the new stewardship program in the parish and implement it.

4. **Implementation Phase:** This is the core of the program, when people actually decide to begin making their offerings to the Lord based upon the stewardship model - using proportional giving/tithe as a starting point. This phase encompasses an entire year - where the stewardship program is implemented and its effects are assessed by the parish leadership and the participants. During this time, there may be some who make their offerings based on the minimal dues system, and others who make their offerings based on the proportional giving model. As the parish engages in stewardship as a model of offering, the leaders must consider how the parish can be faithful to God in the administration of the offerings to God entrusted to the parish through the hands of its members. This 'completes the circle' of the offerings made by the faithful. Key to this administrative process is openness to biblical charity and care for the poor, and responsibilities to central Church administration. Proportional giving by the parish in these areas is important not only because it is effective, but it models proportional giving/stewardship to the entire parish.

5. **Long Term Growth Phase** - As more people are brought into the process, those experienced with the Orthodox stewardship serve as the best witnesses and examples of how stewardship works and renews the life of individuals and the parish as a whole. Over time, stewardship becomes a norm of how the parish and its members view their Christian life. Parish members and leaders become witnesses of how the move to stewardship and proportional giving is not only possible, but life giving. This witness can be provided in an ongoing way by:

- Adult education programs - in depth discussions
- Personal testimonies
- Examples of stewardship at work (e.g. as exemplified in the parish budget)
- Youth programs

Stewardship education must be ongoing, especially in parishes where new members who may not actively practice stewardship as proportional giving arrive on a regular basis.

6. **Milestones** - It is important for leaders to note milestones in the stewardship development process. This affirms the direction/growth of the stewardship effort. Both anecdotal stories and proportional giving family counts can be helpful measures of the penetration of the stewardship message into parish life. Other milestones which manifest the work of the parish ministry and mission are great incentives to continue to grow the stewardship work.

The UOC Office of Stewardship stands ready to support any of our parishes or the faithful members in their efforts to be faithful to God as stewards in carrying out the great mission entrusted to us as members of His Church.

Notes

Preface

[1] For those who may wish to explore the topic more fully, I recommend the seminal work by Anthony Scott, *Good and Faithful Servant,* as an excellent source for additional material for study. Scott's work was integral to much of the stewardship work being done in Orthodoxy today.

[2] The Doctor of Ministry paper is not formally a dissertation, but a *project* hence the term project will be used to describe this work.

[3] When noting the practices of the Orthodox Church in this paper, it will be assumed that the reference is to churches in the United States.

[4] St. Nicholas parish is a mission parish of the Eastern Eparchy of the Ukrainian Orthodox Church of the USA (UOC) under the spiritual leadership of His Eminence Archbishop Antony. I will use the terms 'eparchy' and 'diocese' interchangeably. Any opinions expressed in this paper are my own, and in no way reflective of those of the UOC or its hierarchs, under whose authority I am privileged to serve.

[5] In common church parlance, tithing refers to a practice of offering ten percent of one's income to the Church. However, there are many variations on the practice in Christianity today. My use of the term will refer to a basic ten percent offering of one's gross income to God, through the church.

[6] It has been my contention that a mission parish in Orthodoxy must find its spiritual life from the missionary work of the Church herself and its hierarchy, rather than exist as an independent entity that establishes itself and relies solely on its own resources; eventually vying for formal recognition from some canonically established Orthodox entity for ecclesiastical legitimacy.

[7] Parish dues are a minimum per capita payment set by the church as a requirement for membership. While common, not all parishes have such dues structures and there are many variations on how it is implemented.

8   Among the Slavs, the word *sobor* denotes a church council. In the UOC, the *Sobor* is a triennial convocation of the hierarchs, clergy and lay leadership of the Church for the purpose of setting forth the direction of the Church in the coming years, including its budget. My comments here are my own observations and are made with a profound appreciation of the extraordinary sacrifices of many people (especially our hierarchs) in organizing these gatherings and enabling important issues to be discussed freely and in a spirit of Christian faith. Orthodox Church ecclesiology emphasizes the synergy of the Church, both hierarchy and laity working together in the power of the Holy Spirit.

9   Jas. 1:17. This phrase is repeated in almost every Orthodox Divine Liturgy as part of the Ambon prayer prior to the final dismissal of the congregation. Quotations from the Divine Liturgy of St. John Chrysostom are excerpted from *Molitovnik—Prayer Book*, Permanent Conference of Ukrainian Orthodox Bishops Beyond the Borders of Ukraine (Winnipeg: Ecclesia Publishing and Office of Publications of Ukrainian Orthodox Church of the USA, 2000).

10   These issues are by no means limited to the Ukrainian Orthodox Church of the USA, but exist for all of the jurisdictions in the United States.

11   A concerted effort in a number of the Orthodox Church jurisdictions in the United States has led to the replacement of the dues system in some, and a broader shift toward a stewardship approach. (See Chapter 7) The approach of each is somewhat different from jurisdiction to jurisdiction. While the system of dues has been the basis of funding Church operations in some jurisdictions for decades, revenues from parish dues have declined where the local congregational base has eroded due to the migration of families due to economic concerns and the aging and passing of elderly parish members. See below.

12   The structure of many American parishes—state incorporation with parish lay leadership boards comprised of officers (president, secretary, treasurer, etc.) empowered as trustees—tends to lend a corporate tone to this dimension of parish life. One might wonder whether the first question Jesus asked his apostles when they gathered was, *"Do we have a quorum?"*

13   I would suggest that even where the business model is in place, there are many manifestations of the spirit of Christian generosity also at work. The question is whether or not such a spirit is fostered by the church structures.

14   For the Orthodox, the Holy Scriptures and Holy Tradition have the same origin—the Holy Spirit, and complement one another fully and seamlessly. For a thorough discussion on the interrelationship of Scripture and Tradition in the Church see Timothy Ware (Bishop Kallistos of Diokleia), *The Orthodox Church*. (Middlesex, England: Penguin Books, 1983.). Ware states that, "Christian Tradition . . . is the faith which Jesus Christ imparted to the Apostles, and which since the Apostles' time has been handed down from generation to generation in the Church. Christian Tradition means . . . the books of the Bible; it means the Creed; it means the decrees of the Ecumenical Councils and the writings of the Fathers . . ." Ware, *The Orthodox Church*, 204.

15   In addition to Anthony Scott's work, *Good and Faithful Servant: Stewardship in the Orthodox Church,* Paul Wesche's *The Theology of Stewardship in Light of Orthodox Tradition,* (Minneapolis: Light and Life, 1990) provided an earlier attempt to address the topic.

16   While the scope of theoretical resources is admittedly broad, many aspects of Church life give witness to the practice of stewardship in Church history. For example, the witness of Church architecture and iconography, which is visual in nature, may be more effective for certain people who are visually oriented, in contrast to those who are more verbally attuned to the discussions of Scripture and patristic teaching.

17   This phrase proclaimed during the anaphora of St. John Chrysostom, encapsulates the Orthodox notion of liturgical offering. The Slavonic translation of the phrase "in behalf of all and for all" is "*o vsich i za vsja*". This clarifies the sense that the priestly offering of Christ and the Church encapsulates not only humanity, but all of creation. See *Molitovnik*, 182.

18   In the Orthodox Church, the celebration of the Feast of the Transfiguration (Aug. 6/19) is cause for a celebratory offering of the first fruits of the harvest, typically of grapes. Grapes and fruits are brought to the Church and formally blessed by the priest and shared among the faithful. (Fixed feasts of the Orthodox Church will be

denoted by the Gregorian calendar date followed by a slash (/) then the Julian calendar date.)

19   For the sake of simplicity, this work will focus on material offerings—as these are easier to quantify. It is hoped that the notion of spiritual offerings of other dimensions of the human person can be addressed in another work.

20   From the Greek: *Ortho*—'right', *doxa*—'glory or worship'. Often *doxa* is interpreted as 'doctrine', and while right doctrine and right worship are linked, the translation as 'worship' is preferred here. Translated into the Slavonic, '*pravoslavnij*' is *pravo*—'right', *slava*—'glory'. What the Orthodox Church does on Sunday is the best expression of what it is and believes. In Orthodoxy there exists a unity of the Faith and the expression of the soul in glorification of the God of Truth.

21   'Right worship' = true worship (Gr. *ortho—doxa*) is that which is pleasing to the Father, as described by Christ in his dialogue with the Samaritan Woman (Jn. 4:23). This is the worship 'in Christ' Who is the Truth, and the Head of the Body. (Jn. 14:6). Many ancient anaphoras of Christian eucharistic liturgies begin with the acknowledgment prayer before God, "It is right and true . . . (to offer worship)."

Chapter 1

1   Unless otherwise noted, the use of the term 'man' and masculine terminology where used will include both men and women and will be used irrespective of gender.

2   This might be contrasted with certain dualistic heresies which viewed matter (and the body) as utterly corrupt, and later western theologies that emphasized the depravity of the human condition.

3   Gen. 1, 2. Every year, during Great Lent, the Orthodox Church reads the Book of Genesis liturgically and recalls these fundamental aspects of the human condition in light of the revelation of Scripture.

4   Gen. 2.20. To *name something* is to have a certain position and power of authority. It also implies the capability to circumscribe that which is named—i.e. to understand, embrace and relate wholly to it. Creation is differentiated from God because God is not named by man. (Unless

otherwise noted, biblical quotations are taken from *The Jerusalem Bible,* ed. Alexander Jones, (Garden City, N.Y.: Doubleday & Co., 1966).

[5] The interpretations of the motives of Adam and Eve are many among patristic writers. Generally, the sin takes place because Adam and Eve use creation in reference to themselves alone, and without reference (observance of the commandment and thanksgiving) to God. See the Genesis discussion below.

[6] The anaphora of St. Basil, recounting 'all that was done in our behalf' by Christ, is especially mindful of this, recounting the sending of the prophets and the Old Covenant. For a text of the Anaphora of St. Basil, see *Service Book of the Holy Orthodox-Catholic Apostolic Church.* Isabel F. Hapgood trans., (New York: Syrian Antiochian Orthodox Archdiocese) 1956.

[7] Alexander Schmemann, *For the Life of the World,* (Crestwood, N.Y.: St. Vladimir's Seminary Press, 1973), 17. Schmemann describes humanity as *homo adorans.* This is the very *nature* of human beings, and not obliterated by the fall.

[8] This offering of Christ is salvific because Christ is incarnate—allowing a human sacrifice to again be joined to the divine—in His person.

[9] Anaphora of St. John Chrysostom, *Molitovnik,* 148.

[10] Among the Hebrew terms used to denote offering are *alah* ('to cause to go up'), *zabach* (to slaughter/sacrifice) and *quarab* (to bring near). In the New Testament, the Greek uses terms such as *prophero* ('to bear toward') *anaphero* ('to bear up') and *thusia* (an animal sacrifice).

[11] Gen. 4:1-16. Although the historicity of this event is subject to discussion, the analysis is written as though the conclusions drawn herein are not ultimately dependent upon the events as history. The religious meaning of the passages is clear. A similar approach is taken to those subsequent passages which may also lack certain aspects of historicity. A good treatment of this is presented by Eugene S. Maly in Genesis, *The Jerome Biblical Commentary,* Brown, Fitzmyer and Murphy eds., (Englewood Cliffs, N.J.: Prentice Hall, 1968), 7.

12   It is interesting that this sacrificial action is reported in the Yahwistic account, rather than what one might expect from the 'Priestly' tradition, with its emphasis on hierarchy and cult.

13   The exegesis of the passage leaves room for a number of interpretations as to why the sacrifice may have been unacceptable, including the failure to offer the first and best back to God, the offering of grain verses the flesh of the lamb, the quantity of the offering, etc. I have opted for the first interpretation in light of a number of patristic commentaries (see below) that emphasize the distinction between offering first fruits as juxtaposed to a lesser type of offering. The fat was considered the choice portion of the offering and reserved to God. (Lev. 3:3-5)

14   St. John Chrysostom, *Homilies on Genesis, 18-45*, The Fathers of the Church Series, Robert C. Hill trans., (Washington DC: Catholic University, 1990) Vol. 74, 13. Similarly St. Ephrem the Syrian writes, "Abel selected and offered the choicest of his first-born and of his fat ones, while Cain either offered young grains or certain fruits that are found at the same time as the young grains. Even if his offering had been smaller than that of his brother, it would have been as acceptable as the offering of his brother, had he not brought it with such carelessness." St. Ephrem the Syrian, *Commentary on Genesis*, Ancient Christian Commentary on Scripture, Vol. 1, Genesis 1-11, Andrew Louth, Marco Conti and Thomas Oden, eds. (Downers Grove, Ill: Intervarsity Press, 2001),104.

15   ". . . Cain was very angry and downcast." (Gen. 4:18). In the writings of the ascetic Fathers, dejection (Gr. *lype*) is viewed as a sinful passion that arises in the soul. St. John Cassian describes the demonic force of this passion: "It was this demon that did not allow Cain to repent after he had killed his brother." St. John Cassian, "On the Eight Vices," *The Philokalia, The Complete Text,* comp. St. Nikodimos of the Holy Mountain and St. Makarios of Corinth, ed. G.E. Palmer, Philip Sherrard, and Kallistos Ware, (London: Faber and Faber, 1979), 88. Note also that the Fathers distinguish between *lype* and *akedia* (despondency—often translated as sloth) which are related, but further analysis of these psycho-spiritual dynamics is beyond the scope of this discussion.

16 In other OT passages, notably the sacrifice of Noah (Gen. 8:21) it is clear that atonement can be a component element of acceptable Hebraic offering; it results in the decision by God to never again send a cataclysmic flood. My use of the term atonement will differ from appeasement in the view that to seek 'atonement' means to seek to be 'made one' with God, through humble and obedient sacrificial actions, which are acceptable to God. My use of the term 'appeasement' will refer to a tertiary contemporary use of the term which is to 'make peace' but at the price of principle. In this case, appeasement can be an *a priori* human <u>attempt</u> to act unilaterally so as to deter, defer or bypass the power and judgment of God in a manipulative, rather than a submissive way. Hebrew thought clearly protects the sovereignty of God's power and judgment (and manifestation of His mercy) which cannot be manipulated by humankind, but with which humans live in an ongoing and dynamic relationship. Noah's acceptable offering is made after God's providential deliverance and is part of the unveiling of God's covenant of blessing upon humanity and a renewal of creation. In this sense, the revelation of the mercy of God points beyond atonement in a limited, legal sense toward a sacrificial dynamic of thanksgiving and communion.

17 In the Old Testament, the notion of the tithe is based upon this premise that it is the *first and finest* which is to be offered to God. In the New Testament, Christ would be described by Paul as the "first fruits of those who had fallen asleep." (1Cor. 15:20-23)

18 The Anaphora of St. Basil the Great implores God, " . . . as you accepted the offering of Abel . . . accept these gifts offered by us, sinners." (*Service Book*, 130). This typology is a common hermeneutic of biblical interpretation of the patristic Fathers and, hence, the Orthodox Church.

19 The "land of Nod" means 'wandering'. The Fathers of the Church identified the spiritual state of restlessness as a result of sin at work.

20 One difference in the material nature of the Old Testament sacrifices is that in all cases, the matter of the sacrifices is consumed in flame or by human consumption. In the Resurrection of Christ, the material flesh of Christ is not consumed in the order of natural things. In the Divine Liturgy of Chrysostom, at the fraction of the eucharistic Lamb (consecrated bread), the priest says, "The Lamb of God is broken but

not divided. He is forever eaten, yet is never consumed, but he sanctifies those who partake of Him." *Molitovnik*, 168.

21   Gen. 14:17-24. Melchizedek is king of Salem (Heb. *shalom*—'peace'). Because he comes from Salem, he points to Jerusalem as the locus of the Temple, where the Old Testament sacrifice shall take place. Typologically for Christians, Melchizedek foreshadows the messianic High Priest of the New Jerusalem.

22   See the discussion below, as well as Heb. 5-10 that further develops the themes of the sacrifice and offering by Christ. The Orthodox Church traditionally identifies St. Paul as the author of this letter.

23   Abraham, in the Genesis story, offers to God *through* the ministry of the priest Melchizedek. This might be seen as a foreshadowing of the priesthood of those who, by their participation in this offering dynamic, make their offerings to God through the ministry of those called to offer in behalf of the one who provided the gifts. The action of taking a portion and offering to God (and not keeping it for themselves) is a kind of priestly stewardship.

24   Later, the Levitical priests did indeed receive portions of offerings for their earthly sustenance, according to the order established by God. Likewise, many of the fund-raising efforts done in Orthodox churches are geared to meet special needs.

25   Both the Old and New Testaments emphasize joy as fundamental to a right attitude toward offering. "God blesses a cheerful giver." (Prov. 22.9) and "God blesses the cheerful giver." (2Cor. 9.7).

26   E.g. Mk. 8:36f, Lk. 9:43, Mt. 9:8.

27   On Great Friday, the Orthodox Church celebrates the typology of Isaac, representing Christ, the only Begotten Son, who would not be spared, but rather carry the wood of the Cross bringing salvation to mankind and the birth of a new nation in Holy Baptism. The choice was one of utter faithfulness to God. That the promise embodied in Isaac would be lost in the very act of faithfulness is central to the mystery of this choice where faith transcends mere rationality.

Chapter 2

[1]   Ex. 12:21. In the Greek OT (Septuagint), the term elder would be rendered *presbyteros* paralleling the NT our use of the term 'priest' as the ones empowered to offer the Lamb. Moses is seen as the type of Christ, and this relationship of the type to its fulfillment is directly attested by the apostle John (Jn. 1:17). The Passover Lamb and the Manna from heaven would also serve as types of the Eucharistic offering of Christ, to be shared by the people of the New Covenant. (Jn. 6:48ff)

[3]   Our English term, 'sacrifice' originates in the Latin term meaning, 'to make holy'. The prescriptions concerning the celebration of the Day of Atonement (Lev. 23:26-32), Passover (Lev. 23:4-14), Feast of Tabernacles (Lev. 23:43), etc. all have sacrificial elements. Firstfruits and sacrificial offerings were common in pagan contexts, however the Hebrew offerings differed as they were guided by the Law given by the Lord Himself and other types of offerings which are morally sinful, such as human sacrifice, would be forbidden. Hence the admonition of the leaders and prophets of Israel not to follow the worship practices of the pagans was essential to fidelity to the Covenant and the worthiness of the offerings.

[4]   Christianity would later interpret the elements and manner of offerings symbolically in its worship. Hence, the grain offering would be reinterpreted in the Eucharistic context representing the transformation of grain into bread and the incorporation of the grains of wheat into the Eucharistic Bread of Life (Christ), as early as the *Didache* in the first century.

[5]   The term originates from the Hebrew *maasar* later translated to Greek, *dekate*, meaning 'a tenth.' While accurate measurements became important in Old Testament teachings (Prov. 8:15), the precision of the measurement or mathematical conceptions of earlier civilizations may differ from our own. There were three dimensions of the tithe—those offered annually (for sustenance of the Levites), those offered at the feast (support of the Temple), and the 'third year' tithe (for the poor.) The distinctions between 'tithe' and other first fruits offering were more or less lost after the fall of the Temple and subsequent Christian thought and hence will be used interchangeably throughout this writing.

6   For a detailed presentation, see Michael Prokurat's contribution: "Stewardship and the Tithe in the Old Testament," in Scott, *Good and Faithful Servant,* 27.

7   Note that the locus for the offering is commanded by the Lord as well.

8   The Lord Himself was to be their inheritance. (see Num. 18.2). Note too that the Levites would be impoverished if the tithes were withheld (from God). The theme of support for the clerics from the offerings of the people would also be present in the Christian practice.

9   The *todah (*"thanks offering"*)* of Old Testament had important spiritual implications for subsequent Eucharistic theology, but this cannot be investigated at this point, e.g. 1 Chron. 16:37, 40, Jonah 2:3-10.

10   Christianity would inherit this understanding through the centrality of Jerusalem as the place where, according to Tradition, Adam was buried, Melchizedek served, and Jesus, the New Adam and High Priest, would offer Himself for the life of the world.

11   These principles of spiritual stewardship of the flock are also in effect in the New Testament and the Church.

12   In our contemporary experience of American culture, this communal approach may seem foreign, as we tend to focus more on *individual* responsibility, accountability and judgment.

13   For example, Psalm 19, which paints a picture of the cosmos as God's handiwork, and the psalmist's place within its wonder. The Church has traditionally affirmed the authorship of the Psalms to David himself.

14   This Psalm is integrated into many of the liturgical services of the Church as well as private prayers.

15   That most contemporary commentaries identify verses 16-19 as reflective of a later period (and the restoration of the Temple) does not necessarily unravel the internal connection of the inner sacrifice (repentance) and the outer sacrifice. The external is to mirror the internal.

16   See the discussion of the 'Widow's mite' pericope below.

17   While there is no possibility of treating this topic in any suitable detail here, a very brief discussion of passages which make reference to offerings and tithes in the Wisdom of Sirach, 34-35 is presented below as it was used in the Kievan Church of the eleventh century.

18   Prov. 22:22 – 23:4 gives a typical example of this counsel, "Because a man is poor, therefore do not cheat him, nor at the city gate, oppress anyone in affliction. For Yahweh takes up their cause, and extorts the life of their extortioners."

19   It is recognized that the above discussion regarding the Hebrew scripture is being viewed through the lens of the Christian New Testament and subsequent Orthodox theological development. For example, the understanding of Melchizedek event by the Church is heavily influenced by the typology of the Epistle to the Hebrews as discussed below.

Chapter 3

1   A helpful discussion on temple worship can be found in *Harper's Encyclopedia of Bible Life*, Madeleine and J. Lane Miller eds. (New York: HarperCollins Publishers, 1996), 190-198.

2   Even if Hebrew Christians living in Jerusalem continued to worship in the Temple, by the time of its destruction by the Romans in 70 AD, this would no longer be possible. Full participation in temple worship was unavailable to Gentile Christians as well as to those quite distant from Jerusalem. Hence sacrificial, Eucharistic worship, as instituted by Christ (Lk. 22:19f) in the apostolic communities would allow Christians to fully celebrate and offer the acceptable sacrifice in Christ. (2Cor.9:16)

3   This treatment is admittedly quite brief, hence there is no room to make mention of the Zealots, the Herodians or other groups.

4   Notably, the *Jewish War* by Josephus, writings by Philo of Alexandria, the Dead Sea scrolls, later rabbinic writings and writings by a number of Roman historians. For a useful, general treatment of the topic see the article by Sarah J. Tanzer, "Judaisms in the First Century CE" in *The Oxford Companion to the Bible*, Bruce M. Metzger and Michael D. Coogan, eds. (Oxford: Oxford University, 1993). Another source which

attempts to go beyond the so-called 'elite' forces in Judaic culture at the time, to the life of common people and the disenfranchised of society, is an article by Bruce A. Horsley: "Jesus Movements and the Renewal of Israel" in *Christian Origins*, Horsley, Bruce, ed. (Minneapolis: Fortress, 2005).

[5] For a treatment of the writings of the Dead Sea scrolls and their meaning see: *The Dead Sea Scrolls, A New Translation*, Michael Wise, Martin Abegg, Jr. and Edward Cook, eds. (San Francisco: Harper, 1996). Some believe John the Baptist to have been either a member of the Essenes, although the Essenes are not explicitly mentioned explicitly in New Testament texts themselves.

[6] *The Dead Sea Scrolls*, Wise, Abegg, Jr. and Cook, eds., 204. While drawing upon biblical texts, much of the material in the scrolls is extra-biblical.

[7] Ibid. 126.

[8] There is nothing in the basic orientation of any of these groups that places them at odds with Orthodox Christianity as such. Instead, each tended to emphasize certain aspects of the practice of Judaism at the time. After the conquest by the Romans, Hebraic thought and the emergent rabbinic tradition would be a direct heir to the Pharisee's approach to matters regarding of the Torah and Covenant.

[9] See the online article by James Scott Trimm, "Nazarenes, Qumran and the Essenes" at: http://www.essene.com/History&Essenes/Trimm Nazars.htm. He makes several interesting connections between the life of Paul and possible connections to Essene influences, including the sense of the working of God as mystery. His time spent in Damascus shortly after his conversion may have allowed him exposure to the Essenes.

[10] Helpful writings from this position include: E. P. Sanders: Paul, the Law and the Jewish People, (Philadelphia: Fortress, 1983), J. D. G. Dunn: Jesus, Paul, and the Law: Studies in Mark and Galatians (Westminster/ John Knox Press, 1990) and N.T. Wright: What Saint Paul Really Said, (Oxford: Lion Publishing, 1997).

¹¹ From my understanding of the matter, the Orthodox Church would maintain that certain Pharisees opposed Christ and conspired against Him, leading to His condemnation and crucifixion. In doing so these rabbis may well have misinterpreted their own tradition, to the degree that their teachings based in the Old Covenant were to lead them to recognition of the promised Messiah. Orthodox commentators would have no problem agreeing with the New Perspectivists that the interpretations of Luther and subsequent reformers regarding soteriology are inadequate, but would take a different tack in approaching the question. Such an Orthodox approach to Pauline writings would interpret them in light of the whole of revealed Truth (Tradition), including the traditions of John, Peter, and James in the canonical scriptures as well as the rest of Holy Tradition, rather than in isolation. Very generally speaking, the Fathers of the Church would not utterly reject the Law or the Old Covenant because so much of their understanding of the New Covenant was based on the typological interpretation of the Old Covenant. For Orthodoxy, (as in the Epistle to the Hebrews), the language of ritual and sacrifice is a framework for understanding the saving work of Christ which emerges out of the first covenant. That the Orthodox Church honors Joseph of Arimathea and Nicodemus as saints shows how those who held positions of authority as Jewish rulers (even Pharisees or Sadducees) nevertheless *could* come to know the fullness of the Truth through their encounter with Christ and through faith in Him. The conversion of Paul was another case in point. The use of the phrase "chief priests and scribes" in the gospels seems to portray an alliance of the Pharisees and the Sadducees against Jesus (cf. Jn. 11:47, Mt. 26:3). Again, whether this opposition was universal in the entirety of the Pharisee or Sadducee camps is not evident. Nevertheless, Orthodoxy has historically understood the events of the rejection of Jesus, leading to His crucifixion at the prompting of the Hebrew leadership (representative of the Hebrew people as a whole) as a rejection of the Gospel and the New Covenant in the blood of Christ. This perspective, seeing the whole community as the bearer of the guilt of the leadership, is similar to that of the prophets of the Old Testament, as mentioned above. (Mt. 27:25) While this approach is often misidentified as 'anti-Semitic', it is deeply embedded in the hymnology of the Church, particularly during Holy Week. All people are called to repentance and salvation in Christ—Jew and Gentile alike. Regarding stewardship, the Old Testament images of stewardship would be seen as a *type* to be fulfilled in Christ, and taken to a new dimension

by the ministry of Christ, Who is both kenotic Suffering Servant and Lord.

12   This is the seminal question at the heart of whether or not a tithe is a requirement for Christian life. One's answer will depend on his or her view as to how scriptures are to be interpreted. See discussion below.

13   E. P. Sanders, *Paul, the Law and the Jewish People*, (Minneapolis: Augsburg Fortress, 1985) 19. For Sanders, Paul, sees faith as the bridge of participation to the Gentiles in the faith community which descends from the Covenant with Abraham. There are many voices in response to the New Perspective which defend the standard Protestant approach. For example, see Seyoon Kim, *Paul and the New Perspective*, (Minneapolis: Eerdmans, 1991).

14   For Zechariah's hymn see Lk. 1:67-59. The Magnificat of Mary is found in Lk: 1: 46-55. Interestingly, Mary's faith is in evidence as she sings her hymn prior to the birth, in contrast to Zechariah's doubt, prompting a delay of the hymn until after the birth. The role of faith in thanksgiving and prayer is fundamental. For a detailed analysis of both hymns see Raymond Brown's seminal treatment in *The Birth of the Messiah, A Commentary on the Infancy Narratives in Matthew and Luke*, (Garden City, N. Y., Image Books, 1979).

15   Lk. 2:24. This is done "in accord with the dictate of the Lord", following the Old Testament prescription.

16   See Ex. 13.2ff. This passage serves as the foundation of the Passover commemoration, as the offering of 'the firstborn' is now seen as a remembrance of the deliverance of Israel's firstborn on the night of God's deliverance of the Hebrews from Pharaoh. The Lukan use of this notion of offering may not be accidental, as Christ is the offering of the New Covenant.

17   Lev. 12 1-8. The normal prescription for the offering was a lamb, but two turtledoves were offered "if she cannot afford a lamb." In this scene, the lamb is offered—but the Lamb is Christ. Also of interest, but not quite so relevant to the topic here, is that it is the woman in Leviticus who is to make the offering, not the man, ostensibly remedying her need for purification due to the bloodshed of childbirth. Nevertheless, in the Lukan account, the offering of the child by the mother places

Mary in a unique role as priestly representative of all of humanity. The traditional Orthodox understanding of Mary's virginity during and after birth implies there is no need for her to make an offering for her own purification.

[18] It would simplistic to interpret the whole of the Old Testament in terms that equate the favor of God solely with material wealth, although certain passages could be so read (i.e. the spoils of victories in battle, as in Dt. 2:33-36, Prov. 10:15).

[19] Lk. 6:17-26. In the Beatitudes as presented by Matthew there are no woes pronounced on the rich, the satiated, those who laugh, etc. (Mt. 5:1-10) These themes fomr a basis for much in the Patristic tradition regarding the importance of almsgiving.

[20] The stanzas of the full Kontakion of St. Romanos on the Feast of the Presentation in the Temple reflect on the nature of this offering and encounter. See the annotated translation by Marjorie Carpenter, *Kontakia of Romanos, Byzantine Melodist, I On the Person of Christ*, (Columbia, Mo.: University of Missouri Press, 1970) 35-46. The traditional Orthodox icon of this biblical event places the earthly offerings in the hands of Joseph, but the Son in the hands of Mary.

[21] The prophecy of Simeon regarding the sword of suffering to be experienced by Mary is a foreshadowing of the Crucifixion.

[22] These passages are noted as they appear in the annual Orthodox cycle of Sunday Gospels and hence, are familiar to Orthodox faithful. A review of the Orthodox lectionary reveals a remarkable number (over half) of the Sunday Gospel selections refer to stewardship themes.

[23] While coming from a different (Johannine) tradition during a similar time period, there may be parallels to the judgment of the churches in Revelation who had, to varying degrees, lost their dedication to their "first love" (Rev. 2:7).

[24] The stewardship of Joseph would have been familiar to listeners and the improvement of his standing in Egypt was a sign of God's blessing and *also* Joseph's faithful stewardship.

[25] This hearkens to the original call to stewardship found in Gen. 1. 28ff.

26   Gregory the Great, Homily 18, *A Select Library of Ante-Nicene and Post-Nicene Fathers of the One Christian Church*, P. Schaff and H. A. Wace, eds. (Grand Rapids: Wm. B. Eerdmans Publishing Co. 1955), Series 2 Vol. X, 471-472.

27   Mk. 12:40f. The cleansing of the temple in Mk. 11:15-18 bears a similar theme. The temple was cleansed—not because offerings were unnecessary, but because it had become a 'den of thieves.'

28   Traditional Christian exegesis of these passages posits the judgment pronounced by Christ against of the Pharisees and Scribes as an explicit condemnation of an external religiosity which is divorced from the spirit of the Law (and the love of the Holy Spirit). This is particularly manifest in their disdain for the poor. The condemnation of the Pharisees and Scribes by Christ (and later the apostles) was not pronounced against the practices of offering righteous temple offerings prescribed in the Old Covenant (see the treatment of Luke 2 above) as such. Rather the problem is a cold hypocrisy and self-justification in the heart, exemplified by the behavior of these spiritual leaders, which stands in utter opposition to a humble and righteous sacrifice and to Christ Himself. It is with a similar spirit that Ananias and Sapphira appear to make their offering (see below). It should be noted that this traditional view of the Pharisees is being challenged in certain contemporary biblical commentators (see the discussion of the New Perspectivists above), who view the Pharisees more favorably, as sincerely trying to be faithful to the Covenant and its legal requirements. The legalism to which Christ speaks may be an aberration of what Pharisees actually thought and taught. The condemnation by Christ may have been directed more toward these specific practitioners of an aberrant Pharisaic thought, rather than the interpretive tradition itself.

29   Phil. 2:5-11. This quotation is believed to be an early Christian hymn—placing it in a liturgical, even Eucharistic, context, wherein Paul speaks of the "fellowship in spirit" in the verse preceding.

30   Matthew and Luke indicate there was only one coin; Mark reports the offering as two coins. The coin referred to is a copper coin called a *kodrantes*, worth less than $1 *US* in contemporary value.

31 Mt. 26:14-16. The Orthodox liturgy expends an extraordinary effort reflecting on the betrayal of Judas throughout its Holy Week services. These hymns serve as a warning against avarice and covetousness which lead to utter depravity.

32 The passage points to the dynamic work of the Spirit in the Church and the conviction of the Spirit of Truth at work in the Church to prompt souls to repentance and conversion. To lie to God, Who is present in the Church and to oppose the Spirit is to utterly reject Truth which leads to life and salvation.

33 Several parallels can be found in the Old Testament, including Jos. 7:26 – 8:1, where a curse is placed upon those who covet the spoils of war against God's command and incur His wrath. The rejection of the house of Jeroboam and the destruction of his altar (1 Ki. 11:26-40) and Elijah's defeat of the priests of Baal on Carmel (1Ki 18:20-40) are Old Testament examples of the exercise of God's judgment regarding spiritual sacrifices.

34 It should be noted that the act of "laying the offering at the feet of the apostles" has a somewhat formal, even liturgical sense.

35 The deacons were entrusted with this ministry of care material gifts to be distributed to those in need. (Acts 6:1-6)

36 The primary source for this information is 2Cor. 8, 9.

37 This passage succinctly links the notion of self-offering to God, with ministry of service and the financial offering.

38 Gr. "*charis*" or grace.

39 2Cor. 8:9. This hearkens to the self emptying of Christ (Gr. "*kenosis*") that is reveals the condescension of God in the Incarnation, celebrated in Phil. 2:5ff.

40 Gratitude—Gr. "*eucharistia*" or thanksgiving and "*doxa*"—worship. This terminology is integral to Orthodoxy's most basic tenets.

41 Gr. "*koinonia*". The whole discussion of 'gifts' in the Corinthian community can also be viewed in terms of what Paul says to them

about the gifts of the Spirit in First Corinthians. The gifts of the Spirit manifest the communion of the Spirit.

42   Orthodoxy views these (and similar) passages from an understanding of the importance of human participation in the saving work of God, based on the Incarnation. While humankind was unable to accomplish its own deliverance from sin through its own efforts or works, by being joined to Christ Who has accomplished the redemption of humankind through the Paschal Mystery, the Christian is one who is 'crucified with Christ' (Gal.2:20), 'clothed with Christ' (Gal 3:27), and part of the very 'Body' of Christ (1Cor.12:27). By being so joined to Him, human beings are joined (in time and space) to His eternal sacrifice and restored to communion with God. This grace of a restored relationship is further realized through personal cooperation with the grace of the Spirit, purifying the soul and aligning the totality of the human person to Christ (including the will), in effect accomplishing that incorporation into His Body. Hence salvation is participatory because these cooperative human actions flow from free human decisions that align the person with the divine Will of God. The New Adam, through obedience, heals the rebellion of the first Adam. Participation in the Eucharistic sacrifice in Orthodoxy appropriates to the soul all that Christ has done on our behalf. (See the Liturgy of St. John Chrysostom, *Molitovnik*, 182). Humanity, as the image of God, is invited to generosity as God has been generous.(8:9f)

43   Gr. *"diakonia tes leitourgias"* and *"eucharistian to Theo"*

44   A worthy reflection for the contemporary Church on her mission would be to consider the juxtaposition of temporal aid as accomplished by governments and this spiritual dynamic of charity in the name of Christ, which has much deeper spiritual implications. In an age when charitable institutions established by the Church are being privatized or taken over by government administrators, the spiritual dynamics of true charity must not be lost.

45   Orthodoxy sees this in terms of the Eucharist. For a discussion on the imagery of the Melchizedek references, see the Old Testament treatment above.

46   The soteriological effect of the offering of Christ on the cross was a perfection and fulfillment of spiritual dynamic of the forgiveness of

sins, first set forth by Yahweh in the Old Covenant. This covenantal context is necessary for an understanding of how the priestly language of Hebrews is at once consistent with the Old Covenant and goes beyond it. N.T. Wright observes that, "Keeping the law within Judaism always functioned within a covenantal scheme. God took the initiative, when He made a covenant with Judaism; God's grace thus precedes everything that people (specifically, Jews) do in response. The Jew keeps the law out of gratitude, as the proper response to grace—not, in other words, in order to get into the covenant people, but to stay in . . . Keeping the Jewish law was the human response to God's covenant initiative." N.T. Wright, *What Saint Paul Really Said,* 18. Wright notes the eucharistic nature of the covenantal relationship where observance of the Law was done in gratitude. Elsewhere, he insists on this view of the crucifixion offering within the context of the sin offering of Leviticus. That the words of institution in the ancient anaphoras recall the words of Christ, "Take, eat, this is my Body, which is broken for you for the remission of sins," links the Eucharistic liturgy, from its beginning, to that priestly offering in the Old Testament. The covenant in Christ, however, is a New Covenant, that fulfills and supersedes the Old. See *Molitovnik,* 158.

47 The Church, in its priestly vocation in a restored humanity, continues to offer sacrifice—in the Eucharistic sacrifice (communion with the once-for-all sacrifice of the Lord) and the sacrifice of good works. Both are acceptable and pleasing to the Lord.

48 In some patristic writings, the letter is attributable to the apostle John, in other cases, particularly in the Syrian Church, the Elder was believed to be a certain 'John the Presbyter'.

49 The epistle is believed to be one of the latest works of the New Testament.

50 The language of the acceptance of the missionaries is not unlike similar passages in Pauline epistles where the communities are exhorted to receive the emissaries of the apostle, and ostensibly support them.

51 In the structure of the Gospel of John, this prayer of offering made by Christ is situated as the climax of an extensive narrative (Chapters 13-17) which begins with the washing of the feet and is followed by the passion narrative. It is a Christ's final prayer of commendation of the

Church to the Father and the offering to the Church the possibility of union and communion with God—"That they may be one in us." (v. 21).

[52] Yet we can also say that these offerings fully participate in the offering of Christ, for the Eucharist is an offering and consecration of the elements of the earth as well. The Incarnation assures participation of the material world in the spiritual offering, avoiding a heretical dualism.

[53] Most contemporary scholarship assigns a date to the late first century.

[54] See discussion above regarding the relationship of the early Church to the Pharisees and their practices.

Chapter 4

[1] Because the scope of this study spans two millennia and a variety of cultures, it will be possible to only address these issues in a selective manner. It is hoped that such a cursory review can nevertheless unearth certain aspects of the question that can prompt a more thorough analysis at a later date.

[2] I refer to greatness in the normal usage of the word. Jesus would teach that the greater is the one who becomes the least and the greatest is the slave of all (cf. Mk. 11:42f). Jesus' ministry is that of a servant.

[3] Examples include Lk. 12:42ff and Lk. 16:1ff.

[4] The interrelationship of *oikonomia* and 'care of the household', servanthood and rule/oversight demonstrates a biblical perspective on stewardship that has the Church as a point of reference.

[5] Eventually the term *oikonomia* took on a technical definition as a mode of interpretation and applications of church canons. It is also frequently used to describe manner of God's dealing with the world and humanity in mercy and grace. The term *oikonomos* also came to be used technically to define an official position in the Church for the management of temporal affairs of the Church (see below).

[6] Douglas John Hall asserts that the concept of the stewardship is an important biblical concept that has been misinterpreted over the

ages. He laments, "Rarely does one encounter Christians for whom the metaphor represents a kind of summing-up of the meaning of the Christian life." Douglas John Hall, *The Steward, A Biblical Symbol Come of Age* (New York: Friendship Press for the Commission on Stewardship of the National Council of the Churches of Christ in the U.S.A., 1982), 7.

[7]   From the beginning (Acts 6:1-7) the deacons were ordained by the apostles, and subsequently by the successors to the apostles (the bishops) to provide with the administration of church offerings and their distribution to the poor.

[8]   The terms 'gift' and 'offering' are central to the Orthodox Eucharistic prayer and used repeatedly (in an intertwined way) to denote the Son as the 'Gift' of the Father, the offering of the Son to the Father, the gift of the Holy Spirit which descends upon the people and the gifts of bread and wine, and the material gifts of bread and wine which unite the faithful to the divine offering of gifts. For example, the text of the Anaphora of the Liturgy of St. John Chrysostom has the following translation at the time of the *epiclesis*, " . . . send down your Holy Spirit upon us and upon these Gifts (Ukrainian—*Dari*) set forth before You." *Molitovnik*, 159. This translation uses the term 'offerings' when rendering the phrase, "Remember, Lord, those who *bring offerings (dari prinosjat*'). Ibid., 160.

[9]   In contrast, in the Sunday worship of those Protestant Churches which do not regularly offer the Eucharist, the 'offering' tends to be identified with the financial collection.

[10]   There are several in-depth studies of the broader scope of the topic, including contemporary church practice. For example, see Reuben David Van Rensburg, "Tithes and Offerings in the South African Context, The Bible and Reality", (Th.D. diss., University of Zululand, 2002).

[11]   *The Didache*, Excerpted: http://www.newadvent.org/fathers/0714. htm. The Didache is the earliest known source outside of the canonical scriptures that reports the practices and beliefs of the early Christian Church. It is not accidental that the language of Eucharistic sacrifice and offering is central to its message concerning the meaning of

Christian life. The ministry of the 'prophets' is probably that of the ministers mentioned in the epistle of John above.

12 St. Justin Martyr, in *The Ante-Nicene Fathers, Translations of the Fathers down to A.D. 325*. Vol.1, The Apostolic Fathers: Justin Martyr, Iraneaus, Grand Rapids: Eedrmans, 1981. LXVII, p.185. The Didache has a similar passage. The distribution is reflective of the Eucharistic gifts and, most probably, the foods shared in the agape feast.

13 Justin Martyr, Excerpt from *Ante-Nicene Fathers Vol 1 Irenaeus and Justin Martyr*, P. Schaff and H. A. Wace, eds. (Grand Rapids), from Christian Classics Ethereal Library: http://www.ccel.org/ccel/schaff/ anf01: St. Justin's concern is the reconciliation of the thought and practices of the Old Covenant as fulfilled in the New Covenant.

14 Cyprian of Carthage, Epistle 65, 1. See. Alexander Roberts and James Donaldson, eds., *The Ante-Nicene Fathers*, Vol. V(Grand Rapids, MI: Wm. B. Eerdmans Pub. Co), 367. Cyprian makes the case for the use of the offerings of the faithful in support of the clergy that they might perform their 'divine ministrations' in the manner of the levitical priests.

15 Jerome, as quoted by Brent Walters in The Archivist, "A Patristic Response to Contemporary Issues", August, 1995 (*excerpted from the online edition*: http://www.doctrine.net/tithing.htm)

16 See St. John Cassian, First Conference of Abbot Theonas, Chapter 1 in *A Select Library of Ante-Nicene and Post-Nicene Fathers of the One Christian Church*, P. Schaff and H. A. Wace, eds. (Grand Rapids: Wm. B. Eerdmans Publishing Co. 1955), Series 2 Vol. XI, 503-505.

17 Cassian, *First Conference*, 503

18 Ibid.. Abbot John sees his responsibility as the recipient of the gifts which are to be used for the poor.

19 Ibid,504. This emphasis on free will generosity lies in stark contrast to the spiritual psychology of the dues system in parishes which are coercive by nature.

20 Ibid.

21 Ibid.

22 Ibid., 504f.

23 Ibid. 505. This is a moment of *metanoia* or change of heart that characterizes a Christian's internalization of the life in Christ as it has profound impact on every aspect of human living. Teaching and witness about true Christian stewardship is one way where this *metanoia* can be prompted in the souls of human beings by the power of the Holy Spirit.

24 St. John Cassian goes on to defend the sanctity of marriage and importance of fidelity to the marriage covenant, yet the story of Theonas does pose problems pastorally regarding the counsel of those who feel called to extraordinary generosity when they are yoked in marriage to one who does not share that understanding or calling. Ibid. 507.

25 Financial support of the monasteries tended to parallel that of the churches, however certain patrons might tend to favor the monasteries at the 'expense' of supporting the local church. The distinction between the cathedral tradition and the monastic tradition in Orthodoxy has many facets.

26 "Martyrdom Of St. Victor of Mareseille", from *Butler's Lives of the Saints*, John Gilmary Shea (Benziger Brothers: New York, 1894) excerpt from: http://magnificat.ca/cal/en/saints/saint_victor_of_marseille.html

27 For a description of the functionality of the converted house church, see Richard Krautheimer, *Early Christian and Byzantine Architecture* (Baltimore: Penguin Books, 1975),27-29.

28 See Axel Boethius and J.B. Ward-Perkins, *Etruscan and Roman Architecture, Pelican History of Art* (Harmondsworth: Middlesex, 1970) 152–4.

29 Loosely translated from the Greek: 'the place where the sacred vessels were kept.' The role of the *skeuphylakion* is a subject of considerable relevance to this topic, but cannot be explored in depth here. Robert Taft, in developing the history of the rites of the Byzantine liturgy, refers to the central role of the *skeuphylakion* in the Great Church of Hagia Sophia, in *The Great Entrance: Preanaphoral Rites in the Liturgy*

of St. John Chrysostom, Orientalia Christiana Analecta, 200 (Rome: Pontifical Institute of Oriental Studies, 1978). The most notable example of the *skeuphylakion* is that of the Great Church of Hagia Sophia in Constantinople. As in many other cases of the development of the liturgy and architecture, Hagia Sophia was exemplary, hence imitated widely throughout the empire. A summary of excavations of the *skeuphylakion* of Hagia Sofia was presented by George P. Majeska of the University of Maryland in 1989, entitled "Notes on the *Skeuophylakion* of St. Sophia", at the Fifteenth Annual Byzantine Studies Conference sponsored by the University of Massachusetts at Amherst. An abstract is available on the Internet at http://www.byzconf.org/1989abstracts.html. Another useful resource by Thomas F. Matthews, *The Early Churches of Constantinople—Architecture and Liturgy,* (University Park, Pa. and London: Pennsylvania State University Press, 1977) gives information on the *skeuphylakion* at churches of Hagia Irene, Hagia Theodoros, and others.

30   This practice can be likened to the support of the Old Testament levitical tribe. The funding of the clergy is an extensive topic which intrinsically impacts the issues regarding offering and the Church but cannot be explored in depth here. A useful initial investigation has been produced by Ray Mayhew, "Embezzlement: The Corporate Sin of Contemporary Christianity?" found online at http://www.relationaltithe.com/EmbezzlementPaper.pdf.

31   Canons of the Holy and Altogether August Apostles. in *A Select Library of Ante-Nicene and Post-Nicene Fathers of the One Christian Church,* Series 2 Vol. X,. P. Schaff and H. A. Wace, eds. (Grand Rapids: Eerdmans, 1955).

32   The use of the term 'Byzantine' here is one commonly used and is used henceforth, but hardly accurate as the 'Byzantines' never referred to themselves using the term, but rather Constantinople was called 'New Rome' and the 'Byzantines' called 'Romans' in their day and culture.

33   The evaluation of the evolution of the offerings by the Christian faithful is further complicated by the diversity of practice of the Churches located in the country as opposed to those in the cities. It is easy to assume that the practice in Constantinople was the norm, but it would probably not be true. The variety of principalities and cultures

in the Christian world requires generalization in this exercise when describing such changes over centuries.

34 An earlier comprehensive work in English on the Church-state dynamics of the period was produced by Philip Schaff. *History of the Christian Church*, electronic edition (Oak Harbor, WA: Logos Research Systems, Inc.) 1997.

35 See History of the Christian Church, electronic edition.

36 Charlemagne, "Capitulary for Saxony, 750-800" as excerpted in the Internet Medieval Sourcebook, original text in Boretius, No. 26, p. 68, trans. by D. C. Munro in—University of Pennsylvania. Dept. of History: *Translations and Reprints from the Original Sources of European History*, Vol. VI, No. 5, (Philadelphia: University of Pennsylvania Press, 1900), 2-4. The imposition of the tithe by the Emperor may have indicated the beginning of a shift from a free will offering in a Church context to a tax-tithe to be collected by the state, although still ostensibly for the support and work of the Church.

37 Sir William Tite, "Tithes", in Encyclopedia Britannica, Vol. 11th ed. 1911. Online Edition accessed via www. http://www.1911encyclopedia. org/. The article develops the history of tithing in western Europe and particularly England, through the nineteenth century. The system that developed was quite involved and was well embedded in law. The shift from the understanding that is based in free-will generosity to a "right . . . based upon scriptural precedents" is an ominous one.

38 To a degree, in our own age, secular governments in certain countries continue to support the Orthodox churches, particularly in the former Soviet republics. It will be interesting to chart the new emergence of new paradigms of church-state relations in those countries as they emerge in the coming decades. Schaff (writing in the 19th century) noted this emergence of the American model of Church independence from the state and that "the voluntary system in the support of the church and the ministry which prevailed before the Nicene era, . . . has been restored in modern times in the United States of America." See Schaff, *History*, 61.

39 Schaff gives examples of the extraordinary wealth accumulated in the Churches of the Empire. Schaff, *History*, 65.

[40]   St. John Chrysostom, Homily 21 in 1 Cor. 7, in Schaff, *History*, 61.

[41]   These two needs would not have been pre-eminent prior to the Edict of Milan.

[42]   Krikor Maksoudian, Internet Article "The Armenian Tradition on Gifts Given to the Church, from the Armenian Orthodox Church website, http://www.armenianchurch.org/heritage/history/giving.html

[43]   The economics of the Byzantine state and the Church were complex. The Church tended to find most of its financial support from the nobility, but offerings were still made by other members of the laity to the Church for the breadth of its work. Countless saints accepted the biblical injunction to "Go, sell what you have and give to the poor." and would join monastic communities. The Church and state often worked cooperatively in the administration of goods for the poor. However, I have found no evidence that the Church-state relationship was such that the Church actually collected tithes-taxes on behalf of the state. As with most societies, the wealth of the nobility was acquired through the toil of the poor.

[44]   The donation of the Great Church of *Hagia Sophia* in Constantinople by Justinian comes to mind.

[45]   While it is easy to criticize such donations as displays of wealth and vainglory, in many cases they may well have been offered in the spirit of Christian stewardship. The example by St. Volodymyr is viewed in such terms.

[46]   Volodymyr is revered in Orthodoxy for his charity toward the poor. For an article on the early churches of Rus and information on Volodymyr (and the princes of the period) which they built, see William Craft Brumfield, A History of Russian Architecture. (Cambridge: Cambridge University Press, 1993), 9-15. Upon his death, Volodymyr was interred in this Church, which was subsequently destroyed by the Tartars.

[47]   *Canons of the Holy and Altogether August Apostles,*285. The canon is practical, but also tends to reinforce the spiritual character of the offerings.

[48]   See canon V of Nicea II. *Canons*, 558, 559.

49   See canonical directives to this office (Gr. *ekidikos*) in Chalcedon, Canon II and commentary in *Canons*, 268, 269.

50   The ministry of St. John the Almsgiver, Patriarch of Alexandria, was extraordinary in this regard and worthy of emulation.

51   The use of the term 'Fathers' is in no way meant to lessen the witness of the great 'Mothers' of the Church as well. In terms of Church writings, the vast majority are attributable to men—perhaps due in no small part to cultural biases. Some, such as St. Gregory of Nyssa's *On the Soul and the Resurrection*, were actually composed by women (in this case, St. Macrina) but attributed to men.

52   The monastic saints, by definition, were required to renounce all possessions and owned nothing themselves. The sacrificial charity of St. Nicholas (4th c.) is known around the world to this day.

53   St. Methodius of Olympus, *On Virginity*, Excerpt selected from: http://abbey.suscopts.org/index.php/MONASTIC-LIBRARY/chastity.html

54   St. Gregory Nazianzen, Sermon 1 on Pascha. See *The Paschal Mystery*, Hamman, Adalbert (ed.) Alba House, Staten Island, NY 1069, p. 74. This spiritual focus was a natural fit where the underpinnings of Greek Neo-Platonic philosophy were something of a norm in much of the Greek Christian East.

55   St. Makarios, One Hundred Centuries on Love, *The Philokalia, The Complete Text*, comp. St. Nikodimos of the Holy Mountain and St. Makarios of Corinth, ed. G.E. Palmer, Philip Sherrard, and Kallistos Ware.(London: Faber and Faber, 1979), Vol 3, p. 290.

56   This spiritual interpretation can be seen in tension with that of St. John Cassian, above.

57   St Cyprian of Carthage, Homily on the Lord's Prayer, See. Alexander Roberts and James Donaldson, eds., *The Ante-Nicene Fathers*, Vol. V (Grand Rapids, MI: Wm. B. Eerdmans Pub. Co), 449..

58   See *The Edificatory Prose of Kievan Rus*, William R. Veder and Anatolij A. Turilov, trans. and notations. (Cambridge: Harvard University Press, 1994).

59   The *Izbornik* in Slavonic Orthodox Church life is a book which contains not only liturgical texts, but also writings of spiritual piety and guidance. It was used throughout the history of the Slavonic Orthodoxy as a prayer book and spiritual guide. As such, it reveals multiple sources of Orthodox Tradition—liturgy, scripture, patristic teachings, disciplines, etc. all in one place. The extent copy of the *Izbornik of 1076* is especially significant because it originates so early in Kievan Christianity—believed to be the original written for use in the court of Grand Prince Sviatoslav.

60   Veder, trans., *The Edificatory Prose of Kievan Rus*, 54-56. The *Izbornik* does not use the entire text of *Sirach* and the Slavonic text does not reflect the contemporary order of verses. Despite being a Deuterocanonical book, the fact that *Sirach* plays a prominent place in the *Izbornik* affirms its importance as a source of spiritual guidance in Orthodoxy, and perhaps, the ancient Church in general.

61   'On Charity', *Edificatory Prose*, 10

62   Also significant is that this counsel is reported in the *Izbornik* as spiritual guidance of a lay father to his son. It is an application of the praxis of stewardship in the lay family context, rather than the institutional Church. There is to be consistency between the theoretical teaching of the Church, and its *praxis* in daily life with its profound spiritual dimensions. This teaching is radical to the contemporary Western ear, for it is commonly viewed that frugality in life is a goal, so as to leave a material inheritance for one's family at death. The wise father, with his focus on spiritual treasure, is convinced that God supplies what is necessary for each generation, and implies that subsequent generations will need to lay up spiritual treasures for themselves as well. Hence, he presents the importance of *offering one's family to God*—a total offering not unlike the Widow's mite of the scriptures (see above).

63   Orthodox teaching follows the Greek biblical interpretation of sin in these terms—(Gr.) *hamartia*—"missing the mark." Cf. Lk. 3.3.

64   For example, relative to simony see Canon II of Chalcedon, *Canons*, 268.

65   The parable of the Good Samaritan (Lk. 10:25ff) illuminates the teaching of Christ regarding care of one's neighbor. The answer to Cain's question in Gen. 4, "Am I my brother's keeper?" is Yes.

66   A short summary of some of these works can be found in the footnote to Canon VIII of Chalcedon. *Canons,* 273-274.

67   See the article on the topic by Demetrios Constantelos, "Some Aspects of Stewardship of the Church of Constantinople Under Ottoman Turkish Rule (1452-1800)" in Scott, *Good and Faithful Servant,* 105.

68   This St. John emulated the work of the saintly Patriarch of Alexandria, St. John the Almsgiver, who lived four centuries earlier.

69   Ruth Macrides, "Saints and Sainthood in the Early Palaiologan Period", The Byzantine Saint, Sergei Hackel, ed. (Crestwood, NY: St. Vladimir's Seminary Press, 2003), 69. The *eleos* (oil) was a symbolic term for God's mercy and *eleemosyne* essentially godly charity. The emperor was called *philanthropos basileus,* or "Ruler who loves humankind," the title being quite revelatory of the Byzantine vision of the emperor's call to sacred stewardship. His stewardship was to image Christ—who is the divine *Philanthropos* and *Basileus* in Byzantine Orthodoxy. However, not all the emperors were as exemplary in their living the spiritual mandates of the Gospels. Another useful work which treats the financial stewardship of Church and state in the Byzantine Empire is work by John Boojamra, *The Church and Social Reform: The Policies of the Patriarch Athanasios of Constantinople,* (New York: Fordham University Press, 1993). Boojamra explores certain dynamics between the Byzantine Church and the empire. Of special interest to the stewardship discussion are the aspects of responsibility and roles of the patriarchs *vis-à-vis* the emperors in administration of church and state finances for holy purposes as well the tension between spending to restore of church buildings verses dissemination of funds to assist the poor. Boojamra notes the cooperative work between regional Orthodox Churches, notably the Metropolitanate of Kiev, which would restore the Great Church of Hagia Sophia after an earthquake in Constantinople in 1347, this taking place after the Kievan see had been moved to Moscow (123).

70   The Metropolitanate of Kiev, established in the time of St. Volodymr (Vladimir), would be eventually moved to Vladimir then to Moscow

(1322), however the Church—the *people* of the Kievan Church in what is now Ukraine—continued to be Orthodox. The *Unia of Berest-Ltovsk* (1596) of certain Ukrainian Orthodox bishops with the Roman Catholic Church in lands dominated by Kingdom of Poland further destabilized the spiritual state of Ukrainian Orthodoxy in the region.

[71] The abolishment of the patriarchate in Moscow by Peter the Great in 1700 is an example.

[72] For a thorough treatment of the life of the Church in the Ukrainian lands in this period see Ivan Wlasowsky's, *Outline History of the Ukrainian Orthodox Church*, Vol. 1 and 2, 2nd ed. (Bound Brook, NJ: Ukrainian Orthodox Church of the USA, 1974).

[73] Most of the members of the brotherhoods were laymen, as was their leadership. Originally many of these leaders were renowned for their capabilities as defenders of the Orthodox lands against foreign invaders.

[74] In addition to being a military force for defense of the homeland, these brotherhoods were also defenders of the Orthodox Church and faith in the face of Polish and Latin influences, but most (notably the Lviv Dormition Brotherhood) eventually capitulated to the Latins and subsequently joined the *Unia* in the eighteenth century.

[75] Gr. *Stauropegial* status. This means they are under a bishop who is not the ruling bishop of a territory. This was highly irregular, but deemed necessary. It is also a testimony to the fraternal relationship of the Church of the Ukrainian lands with Constantinople.

[76] Bishop Tikhon (Fitzgerald), to the Diocese of San Francisco and the West, Orthodox Church of America, Oct. 1, 1995. "A Letter of Instruction on the Topic: Honoraria, Fees, "Treby," Emoluments, Gratuities—Money" as reproduced online at: http://www. orthodoxresearchinstitute.org/articles/misc/tikhon_honoraria.htm.

[77] Gregory L. Freeze, *The Parish Clergy in Nineteenth Century Russia: Crisis, Reform, Counter-Reform.* (Princeton: Princeton University Press, 1983) Excerpts quoted from a pastoral letter by Bishop Tikhon of the Orthodox Church of America Diocese of the West.

[78] Bishop Tikhon, "Letter of Instruction", online edition. (Bishop Tikhon's emphasis),. *'Crowning'* is the Orthodox term for a marriage

ceremony, '*Panachidas*' are memorial services for the departed, '*treby*' are offerings for providing services, and '*Moliebens*' are Prayer services for special intentions. It is not clear whether the reason that the faithful themselves did not provide financial offerings to Church in sufficient amounts from which the clergy could derive a living was that they were financially unable to do so, that they were not educated in their faith to know that such offerings were appropriate and spiritually beneficial, or because they simply chose not to do so.

[79] Voluntary offerings to the clergy could be accepted but the clergy of his diocese were to in no way influence the amount of money that was offered or set any standard fee for such services.

Chapter 5

[1] While it could be argued that this discussion is hardly necessary as the theoretical basis for an Orthodox stewardship lies in Scripture and Tradition, a fuller understanding of the American context is necessary to understand how stewardship and leadership patterns emerged in American Orthodoxy that were distinctive to the American experience and, in many ways, less-than-Orthodox. These influences continue in the three centuries since the arrival of Orthodoxy in America.

[2] A fascinating essay on the systematic dismantling of Catholic institutions in England and its effects can be found in the following essay by the UK Heritage Explorer: http://magnificat.ca/cal/en/saints/saint_victor_of_ marseille.html

[3] See Roger Finke and Rodney Stark, *The Churching of America 1776 – 1990: Winners and Losers in Our Religious Economy*, (New Brunswick, NJ: Rutgers, 1992).

[4] Fink and Stark, *Churching*, 17.

[5] It might be instructive for Orthodox readers to recognize the monastic influence on the internal life of the Church. Monasticism creates a 'high tension' force for renewal and a continual, internal source for spiritual renewal in the Church. However, since monasticism is bound canonically to the larger church order, it has (generally) remained a force for internal reform, rather than schism. Similarly the Roman Catholic religious orders were often founded as a result of renewal

forces in Church life, but took on a more institutional structure. Protestantism has no parallel internal structure to deal with the emergence of these new forces of renewal.

6   Ibid. 43. From a theoretical Orthodox perspective, this accommodation of the world is a sign of spiritual dissipation. Orthodox churches are far from immune to these dynamics.

7   The use of the term 'established' denotes those churches that have an official or quasi-official status as a preferred church in one of the colonies (states). Fink and Stark note that the Episcopal Church was established in New York, Virginia, Maryland, North and South Carolina and Georgia. The Congregationalists were established in Connecticut, Massachusetts, New Hampshire and Vermont, and Maine. See *Churching*, 39,40. They describe the disestablishment of the churches beginning early in the nineteenth century.

8   The term here refers to the tax exacted for support of the Church, not a spiritual-voluntary offering. Curiously, in colonial Virginia the term 'tithe' came to be associated purely with a three-tiered taxation system enacted by the General Assembly which provided financial support for the Commonwealth, the local county, and the local parish. Counts of persons for the purpose of per-capita taxation denoted such persons as 'tithables'. Notably, white men and slaves (male and female) were denoted as *tithable* but white women were not. The funds for the parish were administered by the vestry, and were often used for charitable purposes as well the construction of new church edifices. A useful online source that explains the Virginia system can be found at: http://www.virginiaplaces.org/taxes/taxcolonial.html.

9   Frederick Mark Gedicks, "A Two Track Theory of the Establishment Clause", *Boston College Law Review*, no. 5 (2003):45. Note that this 'tithe' system should not be confused with the voluntary offerings to the Church in other eras, for these 'tithes' these were essentially taxes exacted on behalf of the Church-state from the common people.

10   Finke and Stark, *Churching*, 59, 60.

11   Frederick A. Norwood, *Sourcebook of American Methodism*, (Nashville: Abingdon Press, 1982), 379, as quoted by Finke and Stark, in *Churching*, 152.

12 John Wesley, as quoted by William W. Sweet, *Religion on the American Frontier,1783-1850: The Congregationalists,* (Chicago: University of Chicago Press, 1939) as quoted in *Churching,* 159.

13 This loss of dynamism may be related to the a psychological sense of security that sows the seeds of spiritual complacency. Brand new upstart sects have limited material wealth but a strong sense of purpose. This creates a dynamism and energy that has a captivating quality.

14 Finke and Stark name the issue of educated clergy as "one of the most striking differences" between the upstart sects (such as the early Methodists and Baptists) and established churches. By educated is meant formal training in seminary or similar setting, which requires a considerable expenditure of church resources. See *Churching,* 79.

15 The hardships endured by early Methodist 'circuit riders' are the stuff of legend. The sacrifices of the spiritual leaders can spur a sacrificial spirit in others.

16 See Hall, *The Steward,* 40.

17 For a discussion of different theories from a Protestant perspective see Russell Earl Kelly's *Should the Church Teach Tithing: A Theologian's Conclusions About a Taboo Doctrine* (Lincoln, Neb.: IUniverse Inc.,2001). Kelly comes down being against a literal interpretation of tithing texts.

18 For example, Hall is rather harsh in his condemnation of the Church in the Byzantine era: " . . . [F]rom the fourth century onward the great bulk of those who 'become Christian' did so as a matter of course, without any fundamental change of heart (metanoia) or experience of special grace . . . The Church that was inaugurated at the Edict of Milan, unlike the church born at Pentecost, was largely bent upon *self*-service." (Hall, *The Steward,* 36.) Hall is approaching the question in a way typical of many contemporary western commentators, who are not aware of the sacrificial elements of Christian life in the Byzantine period, and beyond. Many were the Fathers of the Church were confessors or martyrs for the faith and led their flocks in self-sacrifice, not self-service. The breadth of Protestant interpretation of the issues of stewardship is based, in part, on the nature of the Reformation itself in removing certain authoritative constraints in the interpretation

of Scripture (such as Church authority and Tradition). In such an environment, many opinions and interpretations arise.

[19]   This tension is reflected in Wesley's comment above.

[20]   As a pastor in a mission parish, I came to know something of the temptation to lower standards for Christian living and Church participation, ostensibly to enable the Church to grow. Making certain accommodations allow the parish may grow numerically for a time, but does not promote spiritual growth in depth and may sow the seeds of internal decay. Usually, these compromises are addressed when people no longer are willing to make sacrifices for the faith. The tendency is to accommodate them—instead of challenging them prophetically to nothing less than the Gospel. The cost of entry is spiritual but also financial, in that the true Christian is called to a sacrificial orientation in all aspects of life.

[21]   A contemporary example may be found in the movement of some mainline Protestant denominations toward inclusion and diversity in certain controversial matters (such as those regarding human sexuality) which have resulted in discontent and even schism. These tensions can be a manifestation of deeply held beliefs and theological positions which sometimes cannot be resolved within the existing structure of the church organization. For those who dissent, their decisions may well be prompted by their desire to exercise good stewardship in the whole of ecclesiastical life. It would be overly simplistic to describe such behavior as an exercise of power through the use of money. Nevertheless, a capitalistic dynamic can be present, as many in financial leadership (Orthodox, Protestant and Roman Catholic) can attest.

[22]   Gary Straus documents the withholding of funds from Catholic Churches by the Catholic laity as a result of the clergy sex scandals in an article titled, "Lay Groups Protest Scandal with Wallets" *USA Today*, Aug. 3, 2002. The sense here is that a capitalistic *way of thinking* is at work—using the currency of money to vote and leverage change.

[23]   From an Orthodox perspective, pragmatism can never be the sole driving force for decision-making in stewardship issues. In his anointing by the woman at Bethany (Mk 14:3-9 and parallels) Jesus teaches that stewardship is not pragmatic in essence. What appeared to the disciples as a waste of worldly treasure was actually a sign of the emerging

Kingdom, which (particularly in Mark) they failed to see. The woman was a good steward of the precious oil but from the fallen perspective of worldliness, she wasted it.

24 John R. Schneider, The Good of Affluence Seeking God in a Culture of Wealth, (Grand Rapids, Cambridge, U. K.: William B. Eerdmans Publishing Company, 2002). In Money, Greed and God, Why Capitalism is the Solution and Not the Problem, (New York, Harper One, 2009) Jay W. Richards argues that policies of governmental programs of 'charity' have exacerbated the problems of suffering and poverty in the world.

25 Schneider, *Good of Affluence*, 39. In this thought process, Schneider is emphasizing that the resultant material riches borne of a faithful spiritual life are a blessing of God, and not necessarily the immediate *goal* of the spiritual life. He insists that Christ identified not only with the poor, but also with other social classes. In doing so, he embraced all humanity. In some ways, this approach seems to be a reaction to liberation theology, with its socialistic political overtones.

26 Ibid.

27 Ibid.119.

28 A number of the discredited televangelists in the 1980s utilized this approach, however it is still quite common. It might be said that this is diametrically opposite of the Orthodox emphasis on *offering*.

29 As an example see Kenneth Woodward's, "Dead End for the Mainline" in *Newsweek*, August 9, 1993, 46-48.

30 Hall, *The Steward*, 38. Ironically, many state Churches in Western Europe are still supported financially by the state, despite the continued decline of active attendance and explicit secularism of their government. Some have literally been converted to museums and supported by the state.

31 Finke and Stark, *Churching*, 139. In calling Catholicism at this juncture a 'sect', they are describing the *sociological* dynamics of Catholicism as a organization at the time—small, dynamic, flexible, and de-centralized. They are not referring to the spiritual character of Catholicism in its full religious and historical context. The first Catholic immigrants

to arrive *en masse* were predominantly Irish; who were encouraged to work on the Erie Canal in the 1830's and began to arrive in far greater numbers as the potato famine deepened in Ireland in the subsequent decade. Other major western European Catholic immigrant groups would not arrive in large numbers until the last two decades of the nineteenth century. Of course, this discussion precludes the prominence of the Catholic presence in Texas, Louisiana and California which had different historical trajectories.

[32]   Ibid.

[33]   See Nicholas Ferencz's treatment in "A Study of the American Orthodox Church and Congregationalism." Ph.D. diss., (Pittsburgh: Duquesne University, 2004).

[34]   Vatican Council II, *Apostolicam Actuositatem: Decree on the Apostolate of the Laity*, In *Vatican Council II: The Conciliar and Post-Conciliar Documents*. ed. A. Flannery OP, Revised edition. Vol. 1, (Dublin: Dominican Publications, 1996) 159-175. This decree, promulgated by Pope John Paul II, speaks to the role of laity, and financial responsibility/stewardship. More recently, Pope Benedict XVI issued the encyclical "*Deus Caritas Est*", (God is Love) that makes mention of the tradition of charity in the early church and calls the post modern Roman Church to the same. An online version in English is available: http://www.vatican.va/holy_father/benedict_xvi/encyclicals/documents/hf_ben-xvi_enc_20051225_deus-caritas-est_en.html. Early in his pontificate, Pope Francis has strongly emphasized the need for a strong Church charitable work orientation.

[35]   It is noteworthy that the new order of the Mass created an entry procession of the gifts into the Church (not unlike the Protestant offering rituals) that is vaguely reminiscent of the Orthodox Great Entrance, except that this presentation is made by the laity to the clergy who receive the gifts at the altar. Some variants include a presentation of financial offerings as well; these are also placed in the altar area.

[36]   Joseph M. Champlin developed such a program which gained widespread use in the Roman Church in the 1980's. See *Sharing Treasure, Time and Talent: A Parish Manual for Sacrificial Giving or Tithing*, (Collegeville, Minn.: The Liturgical Press, 1982). Champlin's program is very much in harmony with Catholic practices such as

the use of offering envelopes, communications to the congregants at Masses, and a programmatic approach that is geared to an audience of those who serve larger Roman Catholic parishes.

37   *Stewardship: A Disciple's Response* (Washington, D.C.: United States Catholic Conference, 1993).

38   Notably, St. Herman of Alaska, St. Innocent and St. Peter the Aleut contributed greatly to the spiritual mission.

39   From its beginning, the Russian missionary work in Alaska and the Pacific Northwest was heavily subsidized by the Mother Church. For a review on the financial troubles of the Russian Metropolia at this time, see the article by John Erickson, "Generosity, Accountability, Vision", in Scott, *Good and Faithful Steward,* 123-124.

40   Because this movement took place primarily within the twentieth century, many of the sources of information for this period are verbal and anecdotal. A few parishes still have founding members within their active membership. A compilation of the oral history of this time could yield a rich understanding of the underlying psychology and spirituality of stewardship practices during this period.

41   For the Orthodox in Greece (under the Ottomans) and the Carpathian mountains (under Catholic principalities), religious freedom was an issue, but not the primary motivation. A good number of immigrants would return home to their native lands once they made enough money in America to provide themselves a decent living in their native land.

42   The term 'Eastern Rite Catholics' is used here to denote those churches (and their members) which adhere to the ecclesiology and doctrines of the Roman Catholic Church and the authority of the papacy, but whose spiritual roots originated in eastern Orthodoxy. These churches broke communion with their mother Orthodox churches as a result of concerted and effective 'reunion' efforts that were conducted by Catholic principalities and Roman Catholic authorities in the Carpathian mountains, in Ukraine and Lebanon in the 16th and 17th centuries. The Eastern Rite Catholic churches tend to follow certain rituals and practices similar to Orthodoxy, but are bound by Roman Catholic ecclesiology and doctrine. The term 'Eastern Rite Catholics' is preferred here instead of the commonly used term 'Uniate' as that

expression, while technically precise, came to take on a pejorative connotation.

[43] Alexis Toth (glorified a saint in 1994) was one of several dozen Eastern Rite Catholic priests who immigrated from Carpatho Rus (western Ukraine) in the 1890's to serve Eastern Rite Catholic immigrant parishes in the United States. Encountering serious resistance from Roman Catholic authorities to his efforts, Fr. Toth sought reception into the Orthodox Church and led a movement to return the Eastern Rite Catholic parishes to the Orthodox fold.

[44] Ferencz states that, "Congregationalism, often called trusteeism, can be defined here as the idea that the authority of the church resides totally within the lay congregation of each parish community." (Ferencz, Nicholas, "A Study of American Orthodox Church and Congregationalism", 3). Obviously, the clergy in such churches are not utterly without authority; however, the exercise of authority by the clergy was often compromised because of the way that the legal structure of the church is constituted. In many cases, a dualism developed between material (lay) and spiritual (clerical) authority.

[45] Eastern Rite Catholic lay congregational leaders fomented the formation of many of the Orthodox congregations at the prompting of priests and lay leaders who followed the rationale of Alexis Toth, who desired the return of the Eastern Rite Catholics to Orthodoxy. In one common scenario, the general parish membership meeting would vote to authorize the lay leadership board to file a lawsuit against the Eastern Catholic diocesan bishop to return the parish property to local parish control. Eventually they would seek an Orthodox bishop or jurisdiction with whom they would affiliate, while maintaining their quasi-independent status.

[46] Generally speaking, these first generation immigrant lay leaders were probably more well off financially than other parish members. In the Slavic communities, these leaders were often at an advantage because they could advocate for the ethnic community in commerce and social interaction, tending to have better language and financial management skills than uneducated laborers. I have known several parishes who routinely elected parish leaders who were successful in the world, but were only nominal in their actual church participation. Ostensibly this was done because the congregation valued a perceived ability by these

leaders to advocate for the community in worldly affairs. This practice is probably not limited to Orthodox parishes.

47   Stories abound of those whose mistrust of central authority in Catholicism would speak of their refusal to "send any of our money to Rome." This tension between clergy and laity may be quite common, but is not universal in churches structured in the congregational model, Orthodox or Protestant. At first, the Eastern Rite Catholics established parishes locally where much of the administration of the parish was handled by lay parish boards. In general, these parishes sought to have an Eastern Catholic bishop of their own. However, when Bishop Soter Ortynsky, the first Eastern Rite Catholic bishop in America, was assigned by Rome in 1907, many Eastern Rite Catholic parishes resisted his efforts to bring all the parishes under a central authority, preferring the quasi-independent status that they had before the bishop arrived. The option to maintain this quasi-independent status was a powerful force in favor of moving the parish back to Orthodoxy, which was, in fact, far less centralized in its administration despite the fact that, in theory, Orthodox theology and ecclesiology places the oversight of the administration of the parishes squarely in the hands of the local bishop.

48   John Erickson, "Generosity, Accountability, Vision", in *Good and Faithful Servant: Stewardship in the Orthodox Church,* edited by Anthony Scott, (Crestwood, NY: St. Vladimir's Seminary Press, 2003).

49   As mentioned above, these brotherhoods were important units of society in Russia and Ukraine in the nineteenth century. In America, the relationship of the brotherhood organization with the parish was often symbiotic. It was not uncommon for the men of the ethnic club to meet in hall of the parish. The social community and the religious community were one.

50   Erickson, Good and Faithful Servant, 121.

51   Ferencz notes that, regarding the Parish Board, "The terminology comes from the original founding of most parishes; civil requirements for incorporation required the establishment of a Board of Trustees to take charge of the parish." *Study of the American Orthodox Church,* 126. Many of the observations in this section are compiled from conversations with priests and laity from a variety of jurisdictions who

expressed their observations and experiences of financial management in their home parishes.

52   This borrowing of Protestant practices was not limited to stewardship. Orthodox church architecture and the introduction of organs were similar developments that made the Orthodox churches appear more 'mainstream' in American society.

53   These chant styles were symbolic of the internal Slavic nationalism identity struggles of these communities, resulting in the distinctive separation of the Carpatho Rusyn congregations and the Ukrainian congregations and separate ecclesiastical jurisdictions.

54   The landscape of those regions of the country where immigrant Slavic Orthodox people settled is dotted with churches which give witness to the *inability* to reach consensus in democratic governance, resulting in divisions, lawsuits and 'new' congregations. The sight of competing Orthodox (and Eastern Rite Catholic) churches side by side or across the street from one another raises an important question about corporate stewardship and Church unity, but validates the 'religious economy' theory of Finke and Stark wherein new, upstart congregations can form from such origins. In such a case, the individual would be called upon to ally him or herself with one of the competing congregations, or sadly, in many cases, the person would choose neither.

55   The choice of the term 'mechanism' is intentional. In the industrial West, there may be a tendency to supplant personal inner spiritual responsibility with a systematic, mechanical and pragmatic approach to such things.

56   To my knowledge, no in-depth, broad based study of the history of the dues system across Orthodox jurisdictions has been undertaken, however it would be most helpful to actually quantify and verify empirically the observations herein.

57   In some parishes, a curious marriage of door-to-door collection and the Ukrainian Christmas caroling tradition took place. The choir would go to the house of both active and inactive parishioners, to sing the praises of the Christmas season and to solicit funds for the parish. This exercise provided much needed funds to pay for the winter fuel bill, and was

generally well received—'lubricated' as it were, by the offerings of food and beverage by the audience.

58   To this day, many nominal Orthodox maintain a payment of dues to the parish so that they can be buried from the Church, with little regard to any real day-to-day engagement with the parish or the sacramental life. Stories abound of those who were not buried from the Church because dues were not paid. The decision to have the funeral of such a person in the Church building was not made by the pastor, based on the person's life of faith, but by the parish treasurer by whether the dues were paid or not.

59   In time, as some immigrant parishioners became successful, or even wealthy, in the American economy. These had no difficulty paying the nominal dues amount. Others, who suffered financial setbacks may have found the dues amount quite difficult to pay, particularly during the Great Depression.

60   The evolution of financial systems in American Orthodox Churches over the last century has been highly uneven from parish to parish. Nevertheless, it can be safely postulated that parish income rarely mirrored the rate of growth of personal income in the time period between the Great Depression, World War II and the postwar boom of the 1950's.

61   Fund raising is not limited to parishes; the monasteries routinely fund their operations through fund raising methods, although usually through the sale of religious items or the produce of their daily work.

62   In some parishes, in addition to dues, parish members were encouraged to donate to specially designated funds (e.g. Building fund, heating bill, church repairs, etc.)

63   This practice is quite solidly in place today, to the point where one pastor informed me that he could raise enough money to make his salary based just on the candle donations to a rather large parish.

64   In many Ukrainian Orthodox parishes, the Ukrainian Orthodox League (UOL) formed local chapters in this tradition and extended its work in many aspects of parish life, including publications and local charity to the broader community. The national Ukrainian Orthodox League

is a recognized as one of the central organizations of the Ukrainian Orthodox Church of the USA, and works to improve the vitality of the Church life throughout the Metropolia. The Philoptochos chapters in the Greek Orthodox Church, and other such groups exist in other jurisdictions in America performing similar functions.

65   In the Ukrainian Orthodox Church of the USA, the annual dues per adult member, as set by the *Sobor*, was $55 in 2005. This is normally forwarded by the parish lay leadership to the Consistory.

66   For example, see the "Minutes of the Finance Committee" of the 17th Sobor of the Ukrainian Orthodox Church of the USA (October 14, 2004), which indicate that the current finance (dues) system was leaving the Church body over $100,000 in the red annually. The treasurer indicated that "drastic cuts" might be necessary to secure a net balance.

67   In one particularly poignant moment when a dying woman was visited by a priest, she *absolutely* insisted that he be paid for the sacramental communion call. She could not be at ease accepting the Gifts, but felt, on some deep psychological level, a need to pay a price for such service.

68   Ferencz, *Study of the American Orthodox Church*, 250.

69   Ibid. 251

70   Scott, *Good and Faithful Servant*, 195.

71   This practice of attesting to the donors of gifts is nothing new. The recent discovery of one of the earliest known Christian house churches (2nd century Palestine) was established based the inscription on the bottom of the table of offering attesting to its donation and giving the name of the donors of the mosaics on the floor. The bottom of the altar has the inscription: "The God-loving Aketous has offered this table to the God Jesus Christ, as a memorial." An online article by Scott Wilson of the Washington Post, "Site May Be 3rd-Century Place of Christian Worship—Discovery Made At Israeli Prison", Monday, November 7, 2005. An online version is available at: http://www.washingtonpost. com/wp-dyn/content/article/2005/   11/06/AR2005110600478.html. The iconography of a number of great churches of Christendom (notably Hagia Sophia in Constantinople) in the first fifteen centuries

attests to the donations of major patrons who are graphically portrayed among the holy ones, making their offering of the Church building to Christ, sometimes in the company of the saints.

72 These are often referred to as 'patronage' of which there are a number of helpful studies in contemporary scholarship in English.

73 Scott, *Good and Faithful Servant*, 196-200. Scott calls legal giving (dues) the "bane of stewardship!" Ibid, 200.

74 Erickson, *Good and Faithful Servant*, 127.

75 These are sociological dynamics at work, which are often opposed to fundamental Christian theology that emphasizes hospitality and welcoming to all, *especially* the stranger. (Gal. 3:28, Mt. 25:35). The process is understandable but not desirable and, in the end, inhibits the capability of the community to reach out to others and to grow. In the end, ironically, the parish that is not growing will often experience financial shortfalls. People seek comfort in familiar communities; ethnicity is a comforting force particularly when one has newly arrived in a foreign land where one does not even speak the predominant language. This dynamic is not unique to Orthodoxy and a parallel might be seen in the formation of parallel communities in other denominations between African American communities and those that were primarily ethnically Caucasian. Often in Protestant Christian denominations in multi-ethnic communities, there are ethnically based church communities easily identifiable by their signs in languages other than English. Immigrants from nations in the Far East often find fellowship and financial opportunities in their local

76 One Orthodox parish priest from a northeastern state reported that the ratio of funerals to baptisms in his parish is about eight to one. The onset of a 'survival mindset' is exceedingly difficult to address; the discouragement and subsequent effects upon stewardship practices among the clergy and laity alike can be palpable in such an environment.

77 Among the Greeks, the *Philoptochos* societies are notable in their broad-based charitable efforts.

[78] The disassociation sometimes results from legal issues regarding tax exempt status of churches, and the inability to offer financial benefit directly to members, which the fraternal organizations could do. As an example, see the history of the Ukrainian National Fraternal Association by Myron B. Kuropas *Ukrainian American Citadel: The First 100 Years of the Ukrainian National Association* (Boulder: East European Monographs, 1997).

[79] Some parishes, by their participation in community ecumenical efforts on behalf of the poor, or in conjunction with other Orthodox parishes, helped to stem the tide of Orthodox isolationism. In recent years, the charitable efforts of various Orthodox Church jurisdictions has resulted in the formation of national and international relief/charity/outreach organizations, such as the International Orthodox Christian Charities and others serving under the guidance of the Orthodox Assembly of Canonical Bishops in North and Central America as well as those created and served primarily by individual Orthodox jurisdictions in the United States. Similarly, FOCUS North America has emerged with a national vision as a ministry to serve the homeless.

[80] In a mission parish context, one can sometimes observe the curious responses of people who come to attend services at a 'church' that doesn't look one if it meets in a rented warehouse or shopping center. Likewise, parish members who move away may not attend an Orthodox parish locally because it is not 'their' church (building).

[81] As one example, a provision exists in the Constitution of the Ukrainian Orthodox Church of the USA for the disposition of Church wealth in the event a congregation itself loses viability. In such strange cases, the parish's money ends up outliving the parish itself. Sometimes lay leaders have argued that these funds should be returned to the remaining parishioners—essentially they propose to receive a windfall from the prior sacrifices of others. Notwithstanding the spiritual audacity of such an action, this process would subject the recipients of such funds to serious Internal Revenue Service penalties due to the violation of federal law, requiring payment of institutional 'back taxes' since the not-for-profit status as determined by IRS would have been violated.

[82] Anthony Scott, "Orthodox America—Philanthropy and Stewardship" in *Good and Faithful Servant,* 192.

83   Candle lighting is an ancient Christian practice but in contemporary Orthodox congregations there is often very little real connection of the lighting of candles and the Liturgy itself. This is evidenced by movement of people lighting candles within the service without regard to the liturgical movements themselves. Many come to the church simply to light candles then leave even though the service continues or during the sermon. In some cases, this behavior is viewed as perfectly 'normal' in Eastern European churches.

84   In most cases the candle and icon concession is innocuous, but it is also not uncommon to run into someone peddling raffle tickets after services or promoting other fund raising schemes. The parallel to the moneychangers in the Temple at the time of Christ should not be altogether lost here (Mk. 11:15-17). However, it can be argued that the narthex *is* to be a place where money is important—as it is freely and generously offered as a first movement of the soul presenting oneself before the Lord in worship. The narthex is the interface between the world and the church.

85   In the ancient Byzantine Church, the eucharistic gifts of bread and wine were accepted and prepared in the *skeuphylakion* and then brought (eventually with ceremony) from the *skeuphylakion* to the altar. This liturgical movement from *skeuphylakion* to altar was a statement of the link between the material gifts offered with the spiritual gifts offered in the Divine Liturgy. There is no such linkage in the Great Entrance of the Liturgy in contemporary practice, where the gifts are prepared by the priest (and deacon) privately in the altar, taken outside in solemn procession into the nave, and then returned to the holy table in the altar. Beyond this liturgical development, with the advent of electronic banking, donations can be automatically deducted from parishioner accounts and forwarded to parish accounts. While convenient for all parties, this technology may effectively eliminate *any* psychological connection of financial offerings made in that manner with the essential Eucharistic context of Orthodox stewardship.

86   For a history of the primary leaders of this movement, see Peter Gilquist's *Becoming Orthodox*, Ben Lomond Cal.: Conciliar Press, 1989.

87   For a detailed analysis of this development see Ferencz, "A Study of the American Orthodox church and Congregationalism". Ferencz maintains that the ancient church practice, upon which Orthodox ecclesiology is

based, rests all matters (spiritual and material) of oversight of the local church squarely in the hands of the bishop. He cites examples, however, of how the very constitutions of Orthodox parishes and dioceses embody the aforementioned dualism. Ferencz, *Study*, 105.

Chapter 6

[1] For example, Fink and Starke cite the Holiness movement in Methodism as an attempt to rekindle the original spiritual direction set by John Wesley. See *Churching*, 163, 164.

[2] For example, Anthony Scott has founded of an organization (Stewardship Advocates) to expand the resources (including Internet resources and presentations) on Orthodox stewardship to the Orthodox churches and groups.

[3] The initial impetus for imposition of a tithe in the seventh century (in the West) came as much from the prompting of the state as from the Church. The Church in the East consistently resisted the temptation to promulgate Christian responsibilities as legal requirements, whereas in the medieval West, the canons became canon *law* which was proactively applied legally to discipline those who strayed. Much of the reaction of the Reformers was to this legalistic framework of late medieval Roman Catholicism.

[4] Cf. Ps. 115. This is a favorite Eucharistic hymn in both East and West. The Gift that God has given is nothing less than the Son, who becomes the Eucharistic Gift.

[5] As discussed above, Orthodoxy does not view the Law or the Old Covenant as a legalistic burden. Rather it is seen an aid by God, to help people direct their lives back to a holy way of living regarding relationships to God, other human beings and creation itself. The Anaphora of St. Basil recounts this, "You gave the Law as an aid, you appointed angels of guardians. And when the fullness of time had come you spoke to us through your Son . . ." (*Molitovnik*, 180)

[6] Many people ask if it's appropriate to base one's proportional offering on gross income or net income after taxes. It is strongly encouraged to base the proportional gift on the former. One needs to simply

ask—do I believe that God should get the first portion of my income, or the government? It might be appropriate to base it on income after subtracting the value of charitable gifts. Better though, is to make the first offering to the Lord, and then make charitable offerings in a spirit of thanksgiving and generosity thereafter.

7   It is easy to be discouraged when we have expectations from others that are not met. In such case we must analyze both how realistic our expectations are and how well we communicated to others the importance of their participation. Even more importantly, we must appreciate each person who does so respond and endeavor to minister without regard to our own preconceived expectations. The gospel teachings of Christ likening the spread of the Kingdom to a mustard seed or leaven in a loaf are instructive.

8   Stories exist of parish treasurers of early American Orthodox Churches reviling and even publicly humiliating people who didn't support the parish 'well enough.'

9   In some cases, the dues were euphemistically called 'obligations', 'offerings', 'minimum pledges', etc. In effect they are a minimum amount that must be offered for a person to be considered a member in good standing. It is effectively 'pay to pray.'

10   Sadly many of the founders and those who supported the parishes during the tough times of the Great Depression have gone to their eternal rest. Many churches exist today only because the faithful mortgaged their homes and sacrificed personal well-being so that the parish could survive financially.

11   A number of small pamphlets have developed on the topic, including a series published by the Orthodox Church of America. These types of works, however, while useful in presenting basic information on a broad scale cannot probe the question deeply. Online sources, including the stewardship offices of Orthodox jurisdictional bodies, are much more readily available.

12   Significant portions of known primary material in Orthodoxy (especially patristic sources) is not yet available in the English language and is scattered throughout many volumes of writings and homilies, rather than in larger single topical works on the subject. While this

work addressed only the typical Eastern Orthodox sources available in English, there is most probably a wealth of material available from African, Armenian, Syriac and other traditions that may be of great value, but not yet available in English. To be fully effective, these resources also need to be translated into the native languages of the Orthodox faithful.

[13] It is the hope of the author to be given the opportunity by the Lord to expand this reflection into another book offering.

[14] The Orthodox understanding of the Incarnation is critical to the formation of a balanced perspective on this issue.

[15] By the use of the term 'tithe' here I mean a voluntary percentage offering, not to be confused with the use of the term as it was co-opted in the Middle Ages to describe money collection systems (taxes) implemented by the church-state complexes, primarily in the West. In each patristic instance cited above (Cyprian, Jerome and John Cassian) the tithe was seen as a worthy practice but not a universal mandate.

[16] Both men and women served as deacons in the early Church; however their ministries were exercised differently. In particular, the witness of the female diaconate in ministering to the special needs of widows and unmarried women can shed light on the importance placed by the early Church on this charitable work.

[17] Ironically, this is a pragmatic reason to jettison pragmatism.

[18] For example, if the parish is declining in membership, there may be systemic issues that need to be addressed and a need for sacrificial giving in the area of hospitality and outreach.

[19] This may seem like stating the obvious, but it is precisely in the fundamentals that Christians and their communities sometimes lose their perspective. The recognition that God is Creator and Source of All (Gen. 1,2, Mt. 5) establishes the fundamental relationship of humans to God as creatures who are created in the image of God. God provides for us all that we will ever need and is the very Source of life. Many sinful excesses (pride, avarice, covetousness, jealousy, etc.) arise from the false belief by humans that they must be providers in some ultimate sense. Here I use the term 'Providence' in a broad, biblical sense—God

as a loving Creator and the One who provides material creation and well-being in an intimate, covenantal relationship—not as it was later used impersonally in Deistic thought.

20 Jas. 1:17. As mentioned above, as the Ambon prayer is recited at the end of the Liturgy, it calls the faithful to an awareness of the Orthodox vision of the world which God has created, and into which they go forth with faith. The Church faithful return, each into his or her own corner of the world, over which they are placed as stewards. As the Liturgy has brought the Church into communion with the Father of Lights, who has bestowed the perfect Gift—the Son—upon His people, so the Church is called to bring the Light of the Faith into the world through their sacred work of stewardship.

21 A helpful exercise for Church administrators would be to take a serious look at where church financial resources are spent. Most likely, material things (buildings) will take up a larger percentage than charities and ministries.

22 This is one operative model in Orthodox catechesis: learning by witness—learning by doing. When theory is put into practice, the Gospel is no longer merely a rational religious exercise of the mind, but a way of life. This awakens a spiritual awareness in the Church, which leads to an imitation of the holy practice. The lives of the saints of old continue to give witness in this way; the lives of the saints of today must do the same.

23 Even Christ was so tempted. See Mt. 4:8-10.

24 St. Paul reminds us that this is nothing less than idolatry. (Col. 3:15) It betrays a lack of trust *in God* and results in spiritual bondage rather than spiritual encouragement. (2Cor. 4:1-2)

25 I have been told by a number of parish members and pastors that bingo had 'built' their church. In some cases it is argued that the social value of bringing people out for bingo provides a needed social outlet for seniors and others. The point is not strong.

26 This happens despite the efforts of church founders, through the dues system, to make everyone's contribution equal.

27   A worthwhile follow-up would be to determine the level of parish and jurisdiction donations to charitable causes as a percentage of income, and compare these to national averages of other denominations. I suspect that much of this charitable work in Orthodox parishes is channeled through national offices of Christian charity in the various jurisdictions—i.e. the Office of Missions and Charity in the UOC—and their targeted campaigns. Another possibility is the relegation of charitable work to the auxiliary organizations (brotherhood, sisterhood, UOL, Philoptochos, etc.).

28   As an example, see the Letter of Diognetius from the 3rd c. See: http://www.vatican.va/spirit/documents/spirit_20010522_diogneto_en.html.

29   See the discussion and notes on St. Theonas, St. Nicholas and St. John the Almsgiver above.

30   The apostles, sent by Christ to minister, also shared in this joy. cf. Lk 10:17-24. Those who go on mission trips with an evangelistic or charitable focus often report a similar experience.

31   For example, if the Church does not dedicate funds to the establishment and support of missions (or if it chooses to allocate available funds to things of lesser spiritual importance), it abandons its fundamental call to share the Good News with those who live areas where Orthodox missions are need.

32   A useful exercise would be to compile the annual budgets of the American Orthodox jurisdictions and determine the percentages of total income dedicated evangelization and charity. "For where your treasure is there also is your heart" (Mt. 6:21)

33   Notably, His All Holiness Patriarch Bartholomew of Constantinople has been a powerful voice in these discussions, which has earned for him the name, "The Green Patriarch."

Chapter 7

1   See http://oca.org/resource-handbook/stewardeducation/an-orthodox-understanding-of-stewardship

2   http://www.antiochian.org/givingcampaign

3   This is not without difficulty, as it seems to make the tithe something other than an offering—to God. The fundamental premise of this book is that tithes and offerings are offerings to God, made in thanksgiving and the tithe represents the 'first fruits' offering.

4   A pledge might be viewed legally as a binding contract. See http://www.perlmanandperlman.com/publications/articles/2008/LegalIssuesRelatedtoUnfulfilledCharitablePledges.pdf

BIBLIOGRAPHICAL RESOURCES

Boojamra, John L. The Church and Social Reform: The Policies of the Patriarch Athanasios of Constantinople. New York: Fordham, 1993.

Burrus, Virginia, ed. *Late Christianity*, A People's History of Christianity, Vol. 2. Minneapolis: Fortress, 2005.

Boethius, Ward and Ward-Perkins, J.B. *Etruscan and Roman Architecture*. Harmondsworth: Middlesex, 1970.

Canons of the Holy and Altogether August Apostles. In A Select Library of Ante-Nicene and Post-Nicene Fathers of the One Christian Church, Series 2, Vol. X, P. Schaff and H. A. Wace, editors. Grand Rapids: Eerdmans,1955.

Carpenter, Marjorie. *Kontakia of Romanos, Byzantine Melodist, I On the Person of Christ*. Columbia, Mo.: University of Missouri Press, 1970.

Champlin, Joseph M. Sharing Treasure, Time and Talent: A Parish Manual for Sacrificial Giving or Tithing. Collegeville, Mn.: The Liturgical Press, 1982.

Charlemagne, "Capitulary for Saxony, 750-800", as excerpted in the Internet Medieval Sourcebook, original text in Boretius, No. 26, p. 68, trans. by D. C. Munro, University of Pennsylvania. Dept. of History: *Translations and Reprints from the Original Sources of European History*, Vol. VI, No. 5. Philadelphia: University of Pennsylvania Press, 1900.

Coniaris, Anthony M. *Where Moth and Rust Do Not Consume: An Anthology on Christian Giving.* Minneapolis: Light and Life Publishing Company, 1983.

Ephrem the Syrian, St. *Commentary on Genesis* Ancient Christian Commentary on Scripture, Vol. 1, Genesis 1-11, ed. Andrew Louth, Marco Conti and Thomas Oden, Downers Grove, Ill: Intervarsity Press, 2001.

Fathers of the Third Century, Hippolytus, Cyprian, Caius, Novatian, Appendix In A Select Library of Ante-Nicene and Post-Nicene Fathers of the One Christian Church, Series I, Vol. V, American Edition, Alexander Roberts and James Donaldson, eds. Grand Rapids, Eerdmans 1981.

Ferencz, Nicholas. "A Study of the American Orthodox Church and Congregationalism." Ph.D. diss., Duquesne University, Pittsburgh. 2004.

Finke, Roger and Rodney Stark. *The Churching of America, 1777-1990: Winners and Losers in Our Religious Economy.* New Brunswick: Rutgers University Press, 1992.

Fitzgerald, Bishop Tikhon. "A Letter of Instruction on the Topic: Honoraria, Fees, "Treby," Emoluments, Gratuities—Money" to the Diocese of San Francisco and the West, Orthodox Church of America, Oct. 1, 1995 online at: http://www. orthodoxresearchinstitute.org/articles/misc/tikhon_honoraria. htm

Gedicks, Frederick Mark. "A Two Track Theory of the Establishment Clause", *Boston College Law Review*, No. 5. 2003.

Gilquist, Fr. Peter E. *Bringing America to Orthodoxy—A Manual How to Begin and Sustain New Missions, and Expand*

Established Parishes, 10th Edition. Santa Barbara, Ca.: The Department of Missions and Evangelism, Antiochian Orthodox Christian, Archdiocese of North America, 2004.

_____ *Becoming Orthodox: A Journey to the Ancient Orthodox Fait,* rev. ed. Ben Lomond Ca.: Conciliar Press, 1992.

Gonzalez, Justo L. Faith and Wealth: A History of Early Christian Ideas on the Origin, Significance and Use of Money. San Francisco: Harper and Row, 1990.

Gregory the Great, St. "Homily 18" in *A Select Library of Ante-Nicene and Post-Nicene Fathers of the One Christian Church*, ed. Schaff, P. and Wace, H.P. Grand Rapids: Wm. B. Eerdmans Publishing Co, 1955.

Grimm, Eugene. Generous People: How to Encourage Vital Stewardship. Nashville: Abingdon, 1992.

Hackel, Serge I. *The Byzantine Saint.* Crestwood, NY: St. Vladimir's Seminary Press, 2001.

Hall, Douglas John. *The Steward: A Biblical Symbol Come of Age.* Grand Rapids: Wm B. Eerdmans Publishing Co., 1990.

Hapgood, Isabel F. trans. *Service Book of the Holy Orthodox-Catholic Apostolic Church.* New York: Syrian Antiochian Orthodox Archdiocese, 1956.

Harakas, Stanley. *Toward Transfigured Life: The* Theoria *of Eastern Orthodox Ethics.* Minneapolis: Light and Life, 1983.

_____Living the Faith: The Praxis of Eastern Orthodox Ethics. Minneapolis: Light and Life, 1992.

Hengel, Martin. *Property and Riches in the Early Church*, Translated by John Bowden. Philadelphia: Fortress, 1974.

Garrett, Duanne E. An Analysis of the Hermeneutics of John Chrysostom's Commentary on Isaiah 1-8 with an English Translation. Lewiston/Queenston/Lampeter, England: The Edwin Mellen Press, 1992.

John Cassian, Saint. Conferences: First Conference of Abbot Theonas, In *A Select Library of Ante-Nicene and Post-Nicene Fathers of the One Christian Church*, Series 2, Vol. XI, ed. P. Schaff and H. A. Wace. Grand Rapids: Eerdmans, 1955.

_____ "On the Eight Vices" in *The Philokalia, The Complete Text*, comp. St. Nikodimos of the Holy Mountain and St. Makarios of Corinth, ed. G.E. Palmer, Philip Sherrard, and Kallistos Ware. London: Faber and Faber, 1979.

John Chrysostom, Saint. *On Wealth and Poverty*, Catherine P. Roth, trans. Crestwood: St. Vladimir's Seminary Press, 1984.

_____*Homilies on Genesis, 18-45*, The Fathers of the Church Series, Vol. 74 trans. Robert C. Hill. Washington DC: Catholic University, 1990.

_____*Sharing Possessions: Mandate and Symbol of Faith*, Philadelphia: Fortress, 1981.

Justin Martyr, St. *The Ante-Nicene Fathers, Translations of the Fathers down to A.D. 325*. Vol.1, The Apostolic Fathers: Justin Martyr, Iraneaus, Grand Rapids: Eedrmans, 1981.

Kelly, Russell Earl Should the Church Teach Tithing: A Theologian's Conclusions About a Taboo Doctrine. Lincoln, Neb.: IUniverse Inc., 2001.

Russell Earl. Should the Church Teach Tithing: A Theologian's Conclusions About a Taboo Doctrine. Lincoln, Neb.: IUniverse Inc., 2001.

Krautheimer, Richard. *Early Christian and Byzantine Architecture.* Baltimore: Penquin Books, 1975.

Kreider, Larry. *Authority and Accountability* updated ed. Ephrata, Penn.: House to House Publications, 2002.

Kuropas, Myron B. Ukrainian American Citadel: The First 100 Years of the Ukrainian National Association. Boulder: East European Monographs, 1997.

Leo the Great, Saint. Sermons 16—19. In *A Select Library of Ante-Nicene and Post-Nicene Fathers of the One Christian Church*, Series 2, Vol. XII, ed. P. Schaff and H. A. Wace, 123-128. Grand Rapids: Eerdmans, 1955.

MacManners, John ed. *The Oxford Illustrated History of Christianity.* Oxford: Oxford University Press, 1990.

Macrides, Ruth. "Saints and Sainthood in the Early Palaiologan Period", *The Byzantine Saint*, ed. Sergei Hackel, ed. Crestwood, NY: St. Vladimir's Seminary Press, 2003.

Maksoudian, Krikor Internet Article "The Armenian Tradition on Gifts Given to the Church", Online article:www. armenianchurch.org/heritage/history/ giving2.

Matthews, Thomas. *The Early Churches of Constantinople: Architecture and Liturgy.* University Park and London: Pennsylvania State University Press, 1971.

Mayhew, Ray "Embezzlement: The Corporate Sin of Contemporary Christianity?" Online at http://www. relationaltithe.com/EmbezzlementPaper.pdf.

McNamara, Patrick H. More than Money: Portraits of Transformative Stewardship. The Alban Institute, 1999.

Milavec, Aaron *The Didache: Faith, Hope, and Life of the Earliest Christian Communities, 50-70 C.E*, Mahwah, NJ, Newman Press (Paulist), 2003

Miller, Madeleinie S. and J. Lane. Harper's Encyclopedia of Bible Life. Edison, NJ: Castle Books, 1996.

Norwood, Frederick. *Sourcebook of American Methodism.* Nashville: Abingdon Press, 1982.

O'Hurley-Pitts, Michael. *The Passionate Steward.* Toronto: St. Brigid Press, 2002.

Ostrogorsky, George. History of the Byzantine State. rev. ed. New Brunswick, NJ: Rutgers, 1969.

Schmemann, Alexander and Kachur, Paul. *Eucharist: Sacrament of the Kingdom.* Crestwood, N.Y.: St. Vladimir's Seminary Press, 1985.

_____ *For the Life of the World.* Crestwood, N.Y.: St. Vladimir's Seminary Press, 1973.

Schneider, John R. *The Good of Affluence.* Grand Rapids: Eerdmans, 2002.

Scott, Anthony, ed. *Good and Faithful Steward: Stewardship in the Orthodox Church.* Crestwood, NY: St. Vladimir's Seminary Press, 2003.

Schaff, Philip. *History of the Christian Church*, Online edition. Oak Harbor, WA: Logos Research Systems, Inc. 1997.

Sider, Ronald J. Rich Christians in and Age of Hunger: Moving from Affluence to Generosity, 20th Anniversary Revision. Dallas: Word, 1997.

Stackhouse, Max. Public Theology and Political Economy: Christian Stewardship in Modern Society. Lanham, Md.: University Press of America, 1991.

Stark, Rodney, The Rise of Christianity. San Francisco: HarperCollins, 1997.

Straus, Gary. "Lay groups protest scandal with wallets" *USA Today*, Aug. 3, 2002.

Sweet, William. Religion on the American Frontier,1783-1850: The Congregationalists. Chicago: University of Chicago Press, 1939.

Taft, Robert. The Great Entrance: A History of the Transfer of Gifts and Other Preanaphoral Rites in the Liturgy of St. John Chrysostom, Orientalia Christiana Analecta, 200. Rome: Pontifical Institute of Oriental Studies, 1978.

Thiessen, Gerd. *Sociology of Early Palestinian Christianity*. Philadelphia: Fortress, 1977.

Tite, William "Tithes", in Encyclopedia Britannica, Vol. 11th ed. 1911. Online Edition www. http://www.1911encyclopedia.org

Van Rensburg, Reuben David. "Tithes and Offerings in the South African Context, The Bible and Reality" Th.D. diss., University of Zululand, 2002.

Ukrainian Orthodox Church of the USA. *Prayer Book—Molitovnik.* South Bound Brook, NJ: Ukrainian Orthodox Church of the USA, 2004.

U.S. Conference of Catholic Bishops. *Stewardship: A Disciple's Response.* Washington D. C.: USCCB, 1993.

Van Rensburg, Reuben David. "Tithes and Offerings in the South African Context, The Bible and Reality", Th.D. diss., University of Zululand, KwaZulu-Natal, South Africa, 2002.

Vallet, Ronald E. Stepping Stones Of the Steward: A Faith Journey through Jesus' Parables, 2nd ed. Grand Rapids: Eerdmans, 1994.

Vatican Council II. Apostolicam Actuositatem: Decree on the Apostolate of the Laity, In Vatican Council II: The Conciliar and Post-Conciliar Documents. ed. A. Flannery OP, Rev. ed. Vol. 1, 159-175. Dublin: Dominican Publications, 1996.

Veder, William. Trans. *The Edificatory Prose of Kievan Rus.* Cambridge: Harvard University Press, 1994.

Walters, Brent, "A Patristic Response to Contemporary Issues", The Archivist, August 1995. online edition: http://www.doctrine.net/tithing.htm

Wlasowsky, Ivan. *Outline History of the Ukrainian Orthodox Church*, Vol. 1 and 2, 2d ed. Bound Brook, NJ: Ukrainian Orthodox Church of the USA, 1974.

Wesche, Paul. The Theology of Stewardship in Light of Orthodox Tradition. Minneapolis: Light and Life, 1990.

_____ "The Patristic Vision of Stewardship." in *The Consuming Passion*, edited by Rodney Clapp. Downers Grove, Ill.: Inter-Varsity, 1998.

Woodward, Kenneth. "Dead End for the Mainline" *Newsweek*, August 9, 1993.

Glory to God in All Things

CPSIA information can be obtained
at www.ICGtesting.com
Printed in the USA
FFOW01n1901021014
7777FF